Cambridge Elements ≡

Elements in Music and Musicians 1750–1850
edited by
Simon P. Keefe
University of Sheffield

MENDELSSOHN AND THE GENESIS OF THE PROTESTANT A CAPPELLA MOVEMENT

Siegwart Reichwald
Westmont College

CAMBRIDGE
UNIVERSITY PRESS

Shaftesbury Road, Cambridge CB2 8EA, United Kingdom

One Liberty Plaza, 20th Floor, New York, NY 10006, USA

477 Williamstown Road, Port Melbourne, VIC 3207, Australia

314–321, 3rd Floor, Plot 3, Splendor Forum, Jasola District Centre, New Delhi – 110025, India

103 Penang Road, #05–06/07, Visioncrest Commercial, Singapore 238467

Cambridge University Press is part of Cambridge University Press & Assessment, a department of the University of Cambridge.

We share the University's mission to contribute to society through the pursuit of education, learning and research at the highest international levels of excellence.

www.cambridge.org
Information on this title: www.cambridge.org/9781009113359

DOI: 10.1017/9781009119610

First published 2023

A catalogue record for this publication is available from the British Library

ISBN 978-1-009-11335-9 Paperback
ISSN 2732-558X (online)
ISSN 2732-5571 (print)

Additional resources for this publication at cambridge.org/Reichwald

Mendelssohn and the Genesis of the Protestant A Cappella Movement

Elements in Music and Musicians 1750–1850

DOI: 10.1017/9781009119610
First published online: October 2023

Siegwart Reichwald
Westmont College
Author for correspondence: Siegwart Reichwald, zreichwald@westmont.edu

Abstract: Drawing on his experiences in Berlin under Schleiermacher and his travels to the Vatican, Mendelssohn, as the Director of Prussian Church Music, wanted to offer an edifying worship experience where large-scale choral works would become an indispensable part of the liturgy, which he saw as a performative or representational act, centered around the life of Christ. Yet he quickly realized that the court and clergy were not interested in his foundational concepts; they merely wanted reforms based on the restauration ideals espoused by Winterfeld and Thibaut. Analyses of his twenty-five Domchor compositions and their revisions in this Element chronicle Mendelssohn's stylistic development and his ability to continue to offer a Christological worship experience within strictly prescribed parameters. The Berlin Domchor and its new repertoire by Mendelssohn and contemporaneous composers quickly became the model for the emerging a cappella movement throughout Protestant Germany.

Keywords: Felix Mendelssohn, Berlin Cathedral Choir, Prussian liturgy, Protestant church music, nineteenth-century a cappella movement

ISBNs: 9781009113359 (PB), 9781009119610 (OC)
ISSNs: 2732-558X (online), 2732-5571 (print)

Contents

1 Back to the Future: Mendelssohn, Berlin, and the Protestant A Cappella Movement

1.1 A Need for Musical Reforms

Protestant churches saw drastic theological, liturgical, and musical changes in the early nineteenth century under Friedrich Wilhelm III, and the Mendelssohn family in Berlin had front-row seats. When Friedrich Wilhelm IV decided to reform the Prussian liturgy further, Felix Mendelssohn was the obvious choice to create a musical language that could match the liturgical reforms. Music was considered the essential and final element of the reforms centered around the Berlin Cathedral. This Element will focus on Mendelssohn's contributions to service music in Berlin and their impact on the emerging a cappella movement throughout Protestant Germany.

Liturgical reforms stood at the end of a broader process that touched on all aspects of Prussian life, from military and politics to economy and culture. The primary catalyst was the Napoleonic Wars. After humiliating defeats, military and administrative reforms brought about Napoleon's defeat. Friedrich Wilhelm III's success allowed him to make more fundamental changes to create a unified postwar Prussia. One example of his reforms is the complete reorganization of the educational system under the leadership of Wilhelm von Humboldt. The founding of the Friedrich-Wilhelm-Universität in 1809 (renamed Humboldt-Universität in 1949) is a tangible result of his reforms.[1] Religion would also play a prominent role in the king's plans.

The first step for church reform was forming the Prussian Union Church in 1817, merging Reformed and Lutheran denominations. Friedrich Wilhelm III's plans for a unified Protestant church met stiff resistance once he started to implement a new liturgy, which he based on attempts by Friedrich Wilhelm I 100 years earlier. The liturgy took elements from Anglican worship, presumed to reflect the church rites of the third and fourth centuries, and combined them with the Lutheran Brandenburg liturgy from 1540. The king's bold aim was to create homogeneity in Prussian worship and offer Protestant worship that, to some extent, predated Roman Catholic liturgy. One of his liturgy's more unusual features was the de-emphasis of the sermon, placed at the end of the service, in favor of ritual. Various subsequent iterations added elements from other Lutheran liturgies and the *Book of Common Prayer*. The liturgy was initially introduced to services in the Prussian army, at the Berlin Cathedral, and the Garrison Church. When Friedrich Wilhelm III recommended its

---

[1] Christopher Clark, *Iron Kingdom: The Rise and Downfall of Prussia, 1600–1947* (Cambridge, MA: Harvard University Press, 2006), 312–344.

adoption throughout Prussia, the so-called Agendenstreit (Liturgical Dispute) ensued.[2]

The theologian and pastor of Trinity Church in Berlin, Friedrich Schleiermacher, played a central role in the Dispute, publishing two anonymous responses under the pseudonym Pacificus Sincerus. He questioned the king's authority in the first and offered a Lutheran viewpoint in the second. The 1823 and 1829 published versions of the prescribed liturgy represent pre- and post-Dispute iterations. Both include simple service music in the appendix. The twelve-page musical index of the 1823 *Liturgie zum Hauptgottesdienste an Sonn- und Festtagen und zur Abendsmahlfeier für die evangelische Kirche des Preußischen Staats*[3] included an Amen, Alleluia, and Sanctus from a Russian Mass, a Saxony Kyrie, and an Agnus Dei from a Swedish liturgy. As with the text selections, the king wanted broad representation. In 1824, the king personally asked for settings by Ukrainian composer Dmitry Bortnyansky at Königsberg and Palestrina scholar and composer Giuseppe Baini, active at the Sistine Chapel.[4] The thirteen pages of music of the 1823 *Liturgie* grew to thirty-seven pages in the 1829 *Agende für die Evangelische Kirche in den KöniglichPreußischen Landen.*

The expanded 1829 musical settings were selected by Karl Friedrich Zelter, Felix Mendelssohn's composition teacher. The appendix consists of various settings of thirteen texts from the liturgy.[5] The simple four-part responses included settings by Bortnyansky and presumably Friedrich Schneider. Zelter had delegated some of the needed compositional work for further settings to his student Eduard Grell, who would eventually work closely with Mendelssohn during his time at the Berlin Cathedral. Laura Stokes has offered a detailed discussion of the Musik-Anhang of the 1829 *Agende*. While the musical responses played an essential part in the liturgy, the settings were merely a vehicle to exclaim the words. No consideration was given to artistic expression; it was purely utilitarian. Furthermore, the *Agende* directed the responses to be sung by a male choir without accompaniment. Stokes concludes that despite the expansion of the appendix of the 1829 *Agende*, "the new church had brought with it not only a divisive new set of liturgical practices, but it had reduced the

---

[2] Anselm Schubert, "Liturgie der heiligen Allianz: Die liturgischen und politischen Hintergründe der Preußischen Kirchenagende (1821/22)," *Zeitschrift für Theologie und Kirche* 110, no. 3 (2013): 293–301.

[3] Liturgie zum Hauptgottesdienste an Sonn- und Festtagen und zur Abendsmahlfeier für die evangelische Kirche des Preußischen Staats (Berlin: Wilhelm Dieterici, 1823).

[4] Schubert, "Liturgie der heiligen Allianz," 306.

[5] Readers can access the [Insert name of the SupMat content] at the following web page [insert URL for online resources].

scope of the musical repertoire tremendously."[6] Friedrich Wilhelm III's new liturgy de-emphasized the sermon, offering instead more ritual that represented a wide range of Protestant, Catholic, and "pre-Catholic" liturgical traditions. Music was literally an afterthought (placed in the appendix) and lacked artistic merit. His son was determined to change that.

Historian Christopher Clark considers Friedrich Wilhelm IV "the last Prussian – perhaps the last European – monarch to place religion at the centre of his understanding of kingship. He was a 'lay theologian on the throne,' for whom religion and politics were inseparable. Long before his father's death in 1840, the crown prince surrounded himself with like-minded Christian friends."[7] From his voluminous correspondence about theology, liturgy, and music with his most trusted advisors, Baron Christian Karl Josias von Bunsen and Count Friedrich Wilhelm von Redern, it is evident how much more import-ance they placed on the role of music in worship. Much of their conceptual framework was based on the work and opinions of lawyer and musicologist Carl von Winterfeld, who championed Lutheran Renaissance composers, in particu-lar, Johannes Eccard, as the models for a proposed a cappella style for the Protestant liturgy while at the same time advocating for the composition of new music.[8]

Mendelssohn quickly became the king's and his advisors' first choice to enact reforms, as they had begun to outline musical reforms and plotted how to engage him:

> With your majesty's character, the difficulty of Felix Mendelssohn's engage-ment, which I have not concealed, will find a simple solution. Were the two current musical positions, Spontini's and Rungenhagen's, not taken, Felix would not wish to have either, probably turn both down, which is what your majesty, as I believe, would prefer. It is about the reintroduction of the most beautiful and noble music into life, as much into the general life of the common folk as into the social life of the higher and highest classes of the most musical and most musically educated people in the world. It seems to me that this can happen through three thus far missing realities:
>
> 1. an outstanding educational institution for all music, in particular, the higher;
> 2. performance of true service music according to your majesty's order;
> 3. performance of great, old and new oratorios – as a future branch of theater productions and already now as part of royal festivities and festivals;

[6] Laura Stokes, "Music and Cultural Politics during the Reign of Friedrich Wilhelm IV" (PhD diss., Indiana University, 2016), 139.

[7] Clark, *Iron Kingdom*, 437.

[8] James Garratt, Palestrina and the German Romantic Imagination: Interpreting Historicism in Nineteenth-Century Music (Cambridge: Cambridge University Press, 2002), 108–113.

Is that not enough for one man and master? I believe it is too much for anybody other than Felix Mendelssohn, and he would also not succeed under another king. Handel would have never become and continued to be the darling of the English nation, had not the ingenious Prince of Wales, George III's father, his oratorios enthusiastically loved, and had the rehearsals not been held in his presence in the Carlton House.[9]

Friedrich Wilhelm IV and his advisors saw the need for far-reaching reforms in church and sacred music, and Mendelssohn was their ideal candidate.

1.2 Director of Prussian Church Music: It's Complicated

1.2.1 Music and Politics: Reform by Committee

Mendelssohn thought he knew what he was getting into. After all, Berlin was his hometown, his siblings were entrenched in Berlin society, and the composer had already left Leipzig for Berlin two years earlier as part of King Friedrich Wilhelm IV's efforts to make Berlin a center for the arts. Yet commuting between Berlin and Leipzig was tiring, and Berlin's failure to create a conservatory had become a reality in Leipzig. Under Mendelssohn's leadership, Leipzig had become one of Europe's most important cultural centers, preserving its glorious past with a J. S. Bach monument and securing its future with an educational institution. Only the king's personal efforts and the prospect of completely reimagining Protestant church music overcame his hesitation – against his better judgment. As Director of Prussian Church Music, Mendelssohn finally had clear directives and would be able to effect groundbreaking reforms. Having been promised a professional choir and orchestra at his disposal, Mendelssohn would be able to write modern liturgical music – true church music. Unfortunately, what was supposed to be the pinnacle of Mendelssohn's musical career turned out to be a slowly unfolding nightmare.

Politics were at the heart of Mendelssohn's frustrations and seeming failure. As various stakeholders pushed competing reform ideals, Mendelssohn could not build consensus around his ideas about church music. As the outsider, he was constantly swimming upstream, fighting the establishment at the Berlin Cathedral at every turn. The value and prominence of music within the new liturgy were the main points of contention. Lack of support from the court left Mendelssohn without clear lines of authority, making it impossible for him to implement or even campaign for church music at a grander scale. As a result, his

---

[9] Josias von Bunsen to Friedrich Wilhelm IV, October 30, 1840; Friedrich Nippold, *Christian Carl Josias Freiherr von Bunsen: Aus Briefen und nach eigener Erinnerung geschildert*, vol. 2 (Leipzig: Brockhaus, 1869), 142–143. (Unless otherwise indicated, all translations are by the author.)

musical reforms shifted to the repertoire for the Cathedral Choir, offering psalms, verses, and a complete mass setting in a modern, highly expressive style that not only enhanced the worship but let the congregation experience worship on a deeper level. Since landmark studies by David Brodbeck, Wolfgang Dinglinger, Laura Stokes, and Julius Reder Carlson have already explored the political quagmire surrounding the liturgical reforms at the Berlin Cathedral, a brief sketch will suffice.[10]

It all began in November 1840, when Ludwig von Massow extended Friedrich Wilhelm IV's offer to Mendelssohn to found and lead an academy for music, which was part of a grand plan for Berlin's cultural development. Having been passed over in 1832 for the directorship of the Singakademie, Mendelssohn was skeptical. Negotiations dragged on for several years, which included relocating to Berlin from July 1841 to November 1842. During his stay in Berlin, Mendelssohn composed *Antigone*, MWV M 12. He decided against permanent relocation but was then offered the post of Director of Prussian Church Music. Further negotiations about Mendelssohn's role at the Berlin Cathedral and the establishment of a professional choir and orchestra made once again slow progress. On October 26, 1842, Mendelssohn met with the king to dissolve his contract. Yet Friedrich Wilhelm IV convinced Mendelssohn to take only temporary leave to Leipzig and to return to Berlin when everything was in place. Mendelssohn agreed and, three weeks later, was named Director of Prussian Church Music.[11]

One year later, on November 25, 1843, Mendelssohn assumed the directorship in person, setting up what Brodbeck aptly called "A Winter of Discontent."[12] On April 10, 1844, only 136 days later, Mendelssohn disengaged from working directly with the Berlin Cathedral. During that brief period, the trajectory of liturgical and musical reforms within the Prussian Union Church was decided, and Mendelssohn was a central player. He would contribute further repertoire for several more years. Most of the behind-the-scenes politicking and negotiating happened behind closed doors. The intensity and acrimony of the deliberations are evidenced by Mendelssohn's avoidance of giving names and details in his letters. Correspondence between his sisters offers some names and details, leaving most things undocumented. We can surmise the difficulty of the task if we consider who the major stakeholders were.

---

[10] Stokes, "Music and Cultural Politics"; Wolfgang Dinglinger, "Mendelssohn: General-Musik-Direktor für kirchliche und geistliche Musik," in *Felix Mendelssohn Bartholdy: Kongreß-Bericht Berlin 1994*, ed. Christian Martin Schmidt (Wiesbaden: Breitkopf & Härtel, 1997), 23–37; Julius Reder Carlson, "Politics without Words: Mendelssohn and His Music in Restoration-Era Prussia (1841–47)" (PhD diss., University of California–Los Angeles, 2015).

[11] David Brodbeck, "A Winter of Discontent: Mendelssohn and the *Berliner Domchor*," in *Mendelssohn Studies*, ed. R. Larry Todd (Cambridge: Cambridge University Press, 1992), 4–5.

[12] Brodbeck, "A Winter of Discontent," 1–32.

As discussed, Friedrich Wilhelm IV was the driving force behind the reforms, together with his trusted advisors, Bunsen and Redern. Bunsen spent most of his career in Rome and London. In Rome, he introduced Mendelssohn to Palestrina scholar Giuseppe Baini and the Papal Choir. Bunsen viewed the Catholic Renaissance repertoire and Anglican liturgy as models for worship in the Prussian Union Church. In 1842, Redern was named Director of Royal Court Music and *Geheimrat* to the king. Both Bunsen and Redern were instrumental in bringing Mendelssohn to Berlin. All three stayed on friendly terms with Mendelssohn during and after his time at the helm of Prussian church music.

Eduard Grell and August Neithardt were the musicians Mendelssohn worked most closely with during his time at the Berlin Cathedral. Grell enjoyed a long career as a church musician and was well established in Berlin. In 1839, he had become the organist at the Berlin Cathedral, and during the winter of 1843/44 he directed the Domchor. As a member of the Singakademie, he had gotten to know the Mendelssohn family. Grell was one of three candidates for the directorship of the Singakademie after Zelter's death. While he received only four votes during the contentious election, he nevertheless became Rungenhagen's assistant and the eventual director.[13] Grell was a strong exponent of early church music and Palestrina's a cappella style.[14] Neithardt had worked as voice teacher at the Domkirche since 1839, became Grell's assistant in 1843, and took over the directorship in 1845. As composers, both had presumably strong opinions about the future of Prussian church music.

Friedrich Strauß and Karl Wilhelm Moritz Snethlage were the main pastors during Mendelssohn's tenure at the Domkirche. Strauß was also the spiritual advisor for the ministry of culture, giving him easy access to the king and his advisors. His book on the church year evidences his direct engagement regarding liturgical practices.[15] While Snethlage was newly hired at the time of Mendelssohn's arrival as a Reformed minister, he presumably preferred a cappella performances of psalms.

1.2.2 Politics and Music: The Questionable Value of Occasional Works

David Brodbeck has chronicled the many obstacles and political intrigues Mendelssohn faced that quickly doomed his reform attempts and cut his tenure short. Read within this context, the Domchor compositions have been

---

[13] R. Larry Todd, *Mendelssohn: A Life in Music* (New York: Oxford University Press, 2003), 265.

[14] Reinhold Brinkmann and Bernd Wiechert, "Grell, (August) Eduard," *Grove Music Online*, 2001; accessed December 10, 2022. www.oxfordmusiconline.com/grovemusic/view/10.1093/gmo/9781561592630.001.0001/omo-9781561592630-e-0000011738.

[15] Friedrich Strauß, *Das evangelische Kirchenjahr* (Berlin: Jonas, 1850).

mostly ignored by Mendelssohn scholarship. Recent cultural studies, however, by Julius Reder Carlson and Laura Stokes have offered more insights into Mendelssohn's brief time at the helm of Prussian church music. Carlson presents a reading of Mendelssohn's *Sechs Sprüche*, MWV B 42, 44, 50, 52, 54, and 55 through the lens of Prussian Restoration politics, suggesting that confessional allegiance "was not merely about faith, but was a structuring fact of modern life inseparable from class, nation, and political creed. In short: given the Restoration conception of 'religion,' Mendelssohn's sacred music may say more about his public relationship with the emerging German' nation' than his personal relationship with God."[16] Laura Stokes delves further into the political, cultural, and political complexities of what she coins "monarchical nationalism,"[17] focusing on Mendelssohn's *Deutsche Liturgie*, MWV B 57. Both studies convincingly contextualize Mendelssohn's work at the Berlin Cathedral, presenting insights hitherto overlooked. Neither study takes a closer look at the repertoire as a whole, as these works seem to have limited artistic value, given their occasional nature. My analyses of Mendelssohn's Domchor compositions will present the other side of the coin, as I will explore the spiritual content in these carefully crafted pieces of church music.

Central to Mendelssohn's reform attempts was the formation of the Cathedral Choir, which was a direct outcome of Mendelssohn's discussions with the king, who wanted to provide Mendelssohn with an "instrument" worthy of his compositional ambitions. Initially, Mendelssohn was promised two ensembles: a choir and an orchestra. But, much to his chagrin, there seemed to be no movement on the formation of an orchestra while the choir was completely reorganized. Under the leadership of Major Einbeck, a choir of twenty-three sopranos, twenty-three altos, nine tenors, and fifteen basses was engaged in March 1843. Up until this point, Einbeck had tried unsuccessfully to create a viable choir. To show a commitment to Mendelssohn's activities, the king agreed to an ambitious restructuring of the Cathedral Choir with an annual price tag of almost 34,000 marks per year: All singers were engaged as professional members of the *Domkapelle*. Grell and Neithardt were put in charge of developing the choir, which would be, according to Einbeck, a well-trained ensemble within a year.[18] The Domchor repertoire, listed in Table 1, reflects the court's limited commitment to focus primarily on a cappella performances.

---

[16] Carlson, "Politics without Words," 92.   [17] Stokes, "Music and Cultural Politics," 5.
[18] Dinglinger, "Mendelssohn: General-Musik-Direktor," 29.

Table 1 Mendelssohn's music composed for the Domchor.

=====

Lobwasser **Psalms**

Modern edition: *Neun Psalmen und Cantique*. Edited by Pietro Cappalà.
Stuttgart: Carus, 1996.

Psalm 24 "Dem Herrn der Erdkreis zusteht," MWV B 34, dated November 13,
1843, premiered December 3, 1843, Biblioteka Jagiellonska Kraków, *Mus.
ms. autogr. Mendelssohn* 38/2, 181.

Psalm 2 "Worauf ist doch der Heiden Tun gestellt," dated November 13, 1843,
Biblioteka Jagiellonska Kraków, *Mus. ms. autogr. Mendelssohn* 38/2, 181–182.

Psalm 93 "Gott als ein König gewaltiglich regiert," dated November 13, 1843,
Biblioteka Jagiellonska Kraków, *Mus. ms. autogr. Mendelssohn*, 38/2, 182.

Psalm 98 "Nun singt ein neues Lied dem Herrn," dated November 13, 1843,
Biblioteka Jagiellonska Kraków, *Mus. ms. autogr. Mendelssohn* 38/2, 182.

Psalm 100 "Ihr Völker auf der Erde all," dated November 13, 1843, Biblioteka
Jagiellonska Kraków, *Mus. ms. autogr. Mendelssohn* 38/2, 183.

Psalm 31 "Auf dich setz ich, Herr, mein Vertrauen," dated November 13, 1843,
Biblioteka Jagiellonska Kraków, *Mus. ms. autogr. Mendelssohn* 38/2, 183.

Psalm 91 "Wer in der Allerhöchsten Hut," dated November 13, 1843, Biblioteka
Jagiellonska Kraków, *Mus. ms. autogr. Mendelssohn* 38/2, 183.

Eight-Part Psalms

Psalm 2 "Warum toben die Heiden," MWV B 41, dated December 15, 1843,
premiered on December 25, 1843, Biblioteka Jagiellonska Kraków, *Mus. ms.
autogr. Mendelssohn* 38/2, 219–228; revised March 1845, Biblioteka
Jagiellonska Kraków, *Mus. ms. autogr. Mendelssohn* 40, 25–33.

Modern editions: *Drei Psalmen*, op. 78. Edited by David Brodbeck. Stuttgart:
Carus, 1997; *Psalmen*, op. 78. Edited by John Michael Cooper. Kassel:
Bärenreiter, 2006.

Psalm 98 "Singet dem Herrn ein neues Lied," MWV A 23, dated December 28,
1843, premiered January 1, 1844, Biblioteka Jagiellonska Kraków, *Mus. ms.
autogr. Mendelssohn* 38/2, 241–267.

Modern edition: *Der 98. Psalm*, op. 91. Edited by R. Larry Todd. Stuttgart:
Carus, 1987.

Psalm 100 "Jauchzet dem Herrn, alle Welt," MWV B 45, dated January 1, 1844,
premiered on January 7, 1844, Biblioteka Jagiellonska Kraków, *Mus. ms.
autogr. Mendelssohn* 39, 43–45.

Modern edition: *Jauchzet dem Herrn (Psalm 100)*. Edited by Günter Graulich.
Stuttgart: Carus: 1990.

Psalm 43 "Richte mich, Gott," MWV B 46, dated January 3, 1843, premiered
February 25, 1844, Biblioteka Jagiellonska Kraków, *Mus. ms. autogr.
Mendelssohn* 39, 47–51; revised March 1845, Biblioteka Jagiellonska
Kraków, *Mus. ms. autogr. Mendelssohn* 40, 39–44.

Table 1 (cont.)

Modern editions: *Drei Psalmen*, op. 78, Brodbeck; *Psalmen*, op. 78, Cooper.

Psalm 22 "Mein Gott, warum hast du mich verlassen," MWV B 51, dated February 1844, premiered April 5, 1844, Biblioteka Jagiellonska Kraków, *Mus. ms. autogr. Mendelssohn* 39, 55–65. In *Drei Psalmen*, op. 78. Modern editions: *Drei Psalmen*, op. 78, Brodbeck; *Psalmen*, op. 78, Cooper.

Six Verses

Modern Edition: *Sechs Sprüche*. Edited by Günter Graulich. Stuttgart: Carus, 1982.

Im Advent "Lasset uns frohlocken," MWV B 54, dated October 5, 1846, premiered November 30, 1846, Biblioteka Jagiellonska Kraków, *Mus. ms. autogr. Mendelssohn* 41, 107–109.

Weihnachten "Frohlocket, ihr Völker," MWV B 42, dated December 15, 1832, premiered December 25, 1843, Biblioteka Jagiellonska Kraków, *Mus. ms. autogr. Mendelssohn* 38/2, 229–231; revised March 1845, Biblioteka Jagiellonska Kraków, *Mus. ms. autogr. Mendelssohn* 40, 35–38.

Am Neujahrstage "Herr, Gott, du bist unsre Zuflucht," MWV B 44, dated December 25, 1843, premiered on January 1, 1844, revised March 1843, Biblioteka Jagiellonska Kraków, *Mus. ms. autogr. Mendelssohn* 38/2, 269–271.

In der Passionszeit "Herr, gedenke nicht unsrer Übeltaten," MWV B 50, dated February 14, 1844, premiered February 25, 1844, Biblioteka Jagiellonska Kraków, *Mus. ms. autogr. Mendelssohn* 39, 52–53; revised March 1845, Biblioteka Jagiellonska Kraków, *Mus. ms. autogr. Mendelssohn* 40, 47–48.

Am Karfreitag "Um unsrer Sünden willen," MWV B 52, dated February 18, 1844, premiered April 5, 1844, revised March 1845, Biblioteka Jagiellonska Kraków, *Mus. ms. autogr. Mendelssohn* 39, 66–67.

Am Himmelfahrtstage "Erhaben, o Herr, über alles Lob," MWV B 55, dated October 9, 1846, Biblioteka Jagiellonska Kraków, *Mus. ms. autogr. Mendelssohn* 41, 110–112.

Miscellanea

Chorale, "Herr Gott, dich loben wir" [*Te Deum*], MWV A 20, dated July 16, 1843, premiered August 6, 1843, Biblioteka Jagiellonska Kraków, *Mus. ms. autogr. Mendelssohn* 38/2, 199–216. Modern edition: *Herr Gott, dich loben wir*. Edited by Roe-Min Kok. Stuttgart: Carus, 1996.

Chorale, "Allein Gott in der Höh sei Ehr," MWV A 21, dated December 15, 1843, premiered December 25, 1943, Biblioteka Jagiellonska Kraków, *Mus. ms. autogr. Mendelssohn* 38/2, 232.

Chorale, "Vom Himmel hoch, da komm ich her," MWV A 22, dated December 15, 1843, premiered December 15, 1943, Biblioteka Jagiellonska Kraków, *Mus. ms. autogr. Mendelssohn* 38/2, 229.

Table 1 (cont.)

"Heilig, heilig, heilig ist der Herr Zebaoth," MWV B 47, composed January
1844, rehearsed on January 24, 1844, Schottenstift Bibliothek, Vienna,
Album Vesque von Püttlingen.
Modern edition: *Heilig* (1844), MWV B 47. Edited by Ralf Wehner. Leipzig:
Breitkopf, 2009.

"Ehre sei dem Vater," MWV B 48, Doxology for Psalm 100, dated January 17,
1844, revised March 1845, Biblioteka Jagiellonska Kraków, *Mus. ms. autogr.
Mendelssohn* 40, 45–46; further revised and transposed for inclusion in *Die
deutsche Liturgie*, MWV B 57.

"Denn her hat seinen Engeln," MWV B 53, composed August 15, 1844, for
Friedrich Wilhelm IV after surviving an assassination attempt, premiered
September 2, 1844, at Königsberg Cathedral, Biblioteka Jagiellonska
Kraków, *Mus. ms. autogr. Mendelssohn* 57, 1–4; revised later for inclusion in
Elijah, MWV A 25.
Modern edition: *Denn er hat seinen Engeln befohlen*. Edited by Günter
Graulich. Stuttgart: Carus, 1996.

Die deutsche Liturgie, MWV B 57, composed October 1846, Biblioteka
Jagiellonska Kraków, *Mus. ms. autogr. Mendelssohn* 41, 93–106.
Modern edition: *Die deutsche Liturgie*. Edited by Judith Silber Ballan. Stuttgart:
Carus, 1997.

1.2.3 A Brief Stint with a Lasting Legacy

While Felix Mendelssohn spent less than five months working directly with
the Berlin Cathedral clergy and musicians, he was nevertheless central to the
establishment of mid-nineteenth-century, eight-part a cappella aesthetics.
Church music and liturgy had always been a part of his spiritual and artistic
experience, and he would stay engaged as a composer for the Berlin Cathedral
Choir for the remaining four years of his life. As a reluctant and oftentimes
frustrated reformer, Mendelssohn helped shape the trajectory of musical aesthetics and liturgical identity of nineteenth-century German Protestantism.
Most, if not all, of the essential elements of the occasional works listed in
Table 1 can be traced back to Mendelssohn's work at the Berlin Cathedral from
Advent 1843 to Easter 1844, revolving around the birth, life, death, and
resurrection of Jesus – the essence of Christian doctrine and worship.
Remarkably, he set aside his own sound ideals in favor of the a cappella
aesthetics held by other stakeholders and helped lay the foundation for the
Protestant a cappella movement that lasted well into the twentieth century.

This Element offers a detailed analysis and contextualization of Mendelssohn's Domchor repertoire. Section 2 offers Mendelssohn's aesthetic and stylistic starting point by exploring his concept of church music leading up to his time at the Berlin Cathedral. His opp. 23 and 39 will serve as specific examples. Sections 3 through 6 follow Mendelssohn's work at the Cathedral from Advent 1843 to Easter 1844. Section 3 looks at music composed for and performed at Christmas 1843 and analyzes the two newly composed eight-part settings, Psalm 2 and the corresponding verse, as Mendelssohn's first attempt to provide a coherent musical and liturgical approach. Section 4 explores the music for New Year's Day within the context of Schleiermacher's theological and practical approach to the liturgy as pastor at Trinity Church, which seemed to have served as a model for Mendelssohn's own ideas about worship. Section 5 traces Mendelssohn's progress as a composer of service music as he is coming to terms with the realization that the reforms are musically and liturgically not as far-reaching as hoped. While revisions of Psalm 43 document Mendelssohn's stylistic development, Psalm 22 shows full mastery of the emerging a cappella aesthetics. Section 6 discusses his exit strategy, which turns out to be a blueprint for generating an a cappella repertoire for worship in the Prussian Union Church. Section 7 traces Mendelssohn's twofold legacy: the impact of the Berlin Cathedral Choir on the emerging a cappella choral movement in Protestant Germany; and the composition and dissemination of an eight-part a cappella repertoire centered around the liturgical year, supplemented by works of Italian and German Renaissance composers and published in various volumes of *Musica sacra*.[19]

2 Mendelssohn's Concept of Church Music

Georg Feder sees the decline in Protestant worship at its low point before and during the reign of Friedrich Wilhelm III with "congregational singing that dragged along laboriously; and impoverished liturgy in which music filled a role of questionable value."[20] Having grown up during that time, Mendelssohn offered this assessment:

> True church music – that is, music for the Protestant Church service, which could be introduced properly while the service was being celebrated – seems to me impossible, and not merely because I cannot at all see into *which* part of the worship service this music can be integrated, but because I cannot *at all* imagine there to be any place for it [in the service]. Perhaps you have something to say that may bring me some clarity, but for now, I really don't know – even if I disregard the Prussian Liturgy, which at once cuts off everything of the kind, and

---

[19] [Various Editors], *Musica sacra* (Berlin: Mortiz Westphal; Bote & Bock, 1839–[ca. 1896]).

[20] Georg Feder, "Decline and Restoration," trans. Reinhard G. Pauly, in *Protestant Church Music*, ed. Friedrich Blume (New York: W. W. Norton, 1974), 376.

which will, probably, neither remain as it is nor go further – how it is to be managed that music in our church should form an integral part of public worship, and not become a mere concert that offers a sense of devotion. This was the case with Bach's "Passion," which was sung at the church as an independent piece of music for edification. As for actual church music, or music for public worship, I know none but the old Italian compositions for the Papal chapel, where, however, the music is a mere accompaniment, subordinate to the sacred functions, co-operating with the wax candles and the incense, etc.[21]

Usually, this excerpt is cited to demonstrate Mendelssohn's broad Romantic understanding of sacred music and his lack of interest in composing liturgical music. But a closer reading will tell us a lot more about Mendelssohn's denominational identity and why he was so hesitant to accept Friedrich Wilhelm IV's offer to reform Prussian church music. It also hints at possible musical solutions for the Prussian liturgy.

Mendelssohn wrote this letter to Ernst Friedrich Albert Baur, a cousin of Mendelssohn's good friend Eduard Devrient and pastor in Belzig near Berlin. It was sent in response to Baur's letter, coauthored by Devrient, which discusses church music in general and then encourages Mendelssohn to write an oratorio about John the Baptist.[22] His comments about Protestant church music are, therefore, about their own denomination, the Prussian Union Church. As discussed above, one of the prominent individuals engaged in this dispute was the theologian Friedrich Schleiermacher, a family friend of the Mendelssohns and the Reformed pastor of the Dreifaltigkeitskirche or Trinity Church, the church closest to the Mendelssohns' residence in Berlin. While we do not know how regularly Felix Mendelssohn attended Schleiermacher's services, it is clear from Mendelssohn's correspondence that he must have attended enough services to have an opinion about Schleiermacher's preaching style:

> It is surely strange, that here in Rome I have become a fan of Schleiermacher; we would disagree less, if we were to get together. For in the Prussian Chapel the pastor, Herr von Tippelskirch, preaches so completely abominably and pathetically, that I find it very nice for today's times to speak so calm and clear as Schleiermacher does.[23]

The addressee of the letter, Julius Schubring, had moved to Berlin in 1825 to study theology with Schleiermacher. He quickly became a regular at the Mendelssohn home, and their friendship lasted for the rest of their lives.

---

[21] Felix Mendelssohn to Ernst Friedrich Albert Baur, dated January 12, 1835; *Felix Mendelssohn Bartholdy: Sämtliche Briefe*, vol. 4, ed. Lucian Schiwietz and Sebastian Schmideler (Kassel: Bärenreiter, 2011), 140–141.

[22] *Felix Mendelssohn Bartholdy: Sämtliche Briefe,* vol. 4, 531.

[23] Felix Mendelssohn to Julius Schubring, dated November 18, 1830; *Felix Mendelssohn Bartholdy: Sämtliche Briefe*, vol. 2, ed. Anja Morgenstern and Uta Wald (Kassel: Bärenreiter, 2009), 133.

Mendelssohn would turn to Schubring for any and all questions related to theology and music. Schleiermacher clearly had been a point of discussion, especially since Mendelsohn presumably also had attended Schleiermacher's lectures at the university.[24]

While Mendelssohn is usually portrayed as Lutheran, his exposure to Schleiermacher, a Reformed minister at the Dreifaltigkeitskirche, points toward a Reformed view. An obvious objection might be that Mendelssohn only chose the Reformed service because of Schleiermacher's prominence and his relationship with the Mendelssohn family as a member of the Singakademie. Yet his baptism by Reformed minister Johann Jakob Stegemann and his theological tutelage under Reformed pastor, theologian, and pedagogue Friedrich Philipp Wilmsen in preparation for confirmation confirm his Reformed background.[25] As a member of the Singakademie, the Wilmsen family had been friends with the Mendelssohns for many years. Wilmsen was pastor at the Parochialkirche, a Reformed church closely tied to the Berlin Cathedral. Under Wilmsen's leadership, his congregation had become a draw for young families, as he was known for his pedagogical skills – in particular, his curriculum for confirmation. Despite their proximity to Schleiermacher's Dreifaltigkeitskirche and the Berlin Cathedral, the Mendelssohns decided to have Pastor Wilmsen instruct their children in the Reformed faith. Another reason for their choice of Wilmsen and the Parochialkirche might have been that Felix's organ teacher, August Wilhelm Bach, was the organist.[26]

Presumably, Mendelssohn's Reformed upbringing not only shaped his views for the rest of his life but might have been a more central part of his identity than has been assumed. Even in Leipzig, the Mendelssohn family chose the local Reformed congregation as their home church over Bach's St. Thomas Church. And, of course, Mendelssohn's wife, Cécile, was the daughter of a French Huguenot pastor. When the king asked Mendelssohn to lead Prussian church music, he knew what he was getting into. He surely had followed Schleiermacher's involvement with the Agendenstreit and understood the issues. It was presumably precisely because of his Reformed background that he might have felt a sense of duty to participate in the reform attempts.

Beyond a clear understanding of his Reformed tradition, Mendelssohn's exposure to Catholic liturgy is evident from the second half of his "Credo" on church music. Mendelssohn had spent several months in Rome, not only eagerly attending services at the Papal Chapel, but also becoming friends with

---

[24] Todd, Mendelssohn: A Life in Music, 198.   [25] Todd, Mendelssohn: A Life in Music, 33.

[26] Martin Staehelin, "Der frühreife Felix Mendelssohn Bartholdy: Bemerkungen zu seinem 'Konfirmationsbekenntnis,'" in *Mendelssohn-Studien*, vol. 16, ed. Hans-Günter Klein and Christoph Schulte (Hannover: Wehrhahn, 2009), 11–49.

Palestrina scholar Giuseppe Baini and other members of the Papal Choir. He had become an insider and deeply appreciated Catholic liturgy and its music. Mendelssohn had also been aware of the back-to-Palestrina movement, as championed by Justus Thibaut (whom he had visited while a student in Berlin) and Bunsen, a friend from his time in Rome.[27] It is easy to understand why the king was keen on getting Mendelssohn involved in his reform attempts. However, Mendelssohn was not so keen on the Catholic Palestrina model, stating that "the music is a mere accompaniment, subordinate to the sacred functions, co-operating with the wax candles and the incense, etc."[28] In Mendelssohn's mind, true church music should play a more prominent role in worship.

What did Mendelssohn consider to be modern church music? A look at his oeuvre of published sacred works leading up to his work at the Berlin Cathedral will offer some insights. Mendelssohn's op. 23, his first publication of sacred music, bore the title *Kirchenmusik* ("Church Music"), showcasing his broad understanding of the term. The three pieces are neither liturgical nor intended for worship, as they were composed with the Berlin Singakademie and Frankfurt Cäcilienverein in mind. The compositions espouse Romantic expression, in both style and autobiographic meaning. Written during the Grand Tour of Italy, Mendelssohn explored a wide range of Catholic and Lutheran styles that represent his exposure to Catholicism. At the same time, they are markers of a broadening view on music and religion.[29]

Why did he call them *Kirchenmusik*? Presumably because each piece offers a modern version of "the old" styles – both Protestant and Catholic. *Aus tiefer Not*, MWV 20, is a chorale cantata, the *Ave Maria*, MWV B 19, an offertorium, and *Mitten wir im Leben sind*, MWV B 21, a chorale motet. *Mitten wir im Leben sind* is easily the most "liturgical" and modern in character. James Garratt suggests that "the chorale portions of the work reflect not the style of Bach's harmonizations, but the nineteenth-century 'reformed' chorale, the return to the supposed simplicity and suitability advocated by Thibaut and, among others, Mendelssohn's organ teacher August Wilhelm Bach (1796–1869). There is a reciprocal relation between early nineteenth-century ideas on chorale reform and the idealization of old Italian homophony."[30] In other words, Mendelssohn used the styles of Palestrina and Bach as reference points for a modern

[27] Siegwart Reichwald, "Mendelssohn and the Catholic Tradition: Roman Influences on His Kirchen-Musik, Op. 23 and Drei Motetten, Op. 39," in *Mendelssohn, the Organ, and the Music of the Past*, ed. Jürgen Thym (Rochester, NY: University of Rochester Press, 2014), 42.

[28] Felix Mendelssohn to Ernst Friedrich Albert Baur, dated January 12, 1835; *Felix Mendelssohn Bartholdy: Sämtliche Briefe*, vol. 4, 141.

[29] Reichwald, "Mendelssohn and the Catholic Tradition," 43–48.

[30] Garratt, *Palestrina and the German Romantic Imagination*, 63.

eight-part a cappella style informed by the latest reform ideals of Thibault and Winterfeld.

Mendelssohn's *Aus tiefer Not*, however, goes far beyond the back-to-Palestrina aesthetic. Its essence is rooted in Romanticism, as the composer himself explains:

> open a hymnbook to the following: "Mitten wir im Leben sind" or "Aus tiefer Not" or "Vom Himmel hoch, da komm ich her," "Ach, Gott vom Himmel sieh darein," "Mit Fried' und Freud," in short, all of them. How every word calls for music, how every stanza is a different piece, how one finds progression, movement, growth; it is just too wonderful, and so I work in the middle of Rome diligently on them and visit the cloister where he [Luther] lived and witnessed the mad spectacle of the clergymen.[31]

Mendelssohn equates Luther's chorales with poetic texts that demand music with great immediacy. He seems to be less concerned about contrapuntal ideals or stylistic models; rather, his focus is on expressing the words as directly as possible. The styles have been internalized and have become part of his Romantic language.[32]

Other than the opening line, *Mitten wir im Leben sind* is freely composed. Mendelssohn nevertheless followed the textual division of three stanzas and refrain in his three-part design: A-A'-A."[33] Mendelssohn's own concise musical description in a letter to his sisters covers the basic design for each stanza well: "I have once again a new chorale for the Sing-Akademie: 'In the midst of life we are surrounded by death, therefore we search for who can provide help to us poor people in the time of need?' That's asked by the male voices, and then enter the female voices *piano*: 'you alone, Lord, provide.' Then there is wicked noise and at the end 'Kyrie eleison.'"[34] Mendelssohn uses the eight-part texture to create a sense of drama, as he offers his interpretation of the text. In another letter he calls this chorale motet "one of the best church music pieces I have produced, and it growls wickedly and whistles dark blue."[35] Brahms seems to have concurred with Mendelssohn's assessment. Not only did he perform *Mitten wir in Leben sind* at concert of the Vienna Singakademie in 1864, he even acquired the autograph.[36]

---

[31] Felix Mendelssohn to Carl Klingemann, dated December 26, 1830; *Felix Mendelssohn Bartholdy: Sämtliche Briefe*, vol. 2, 184.

[32] Reichwald, "Mendelssohn and the Catholic Tradition," 47.   [33] See website for score.

[34] Felix Mendelssohn to Fanny Hensel and Rebecka Mendelssohn, dated October 23, 1830; *Felix Mendelssohn Bartholdy: Sämtliche Briefe*, vol. 2, 115–116.

[35] Felix Mendelssohn to Fanny Hensel and Rebecka Mendelssohn, dated November 23, 1830; *Felix Mendelssohn Bartholdy: Sämtliche Briefe*, vol. 2, 139.

[36] David Brodbeck, "Brahms's Mendelssohn," in *Brahms Studies*, vol. 2, ed. David Brodbeck (Lincoln, NE: University of Nebraska Press, 1998), 210–211, 214.

When Mendelssohn penned his "Credo" from Catholic Düsseldorf, several years after the op. 23 publication, he was in the middle of composing his first oratorio, *Paulus*. To him, *Paulus* also represents church music: music for edification but with no liturgical function, music that turns every room into a church.[37] Mendelssohn's portrayal of the apostle Paul goes far beyond story-telling. He wants the audience to understand the theological and cultural implications of Paul's ministry in a genuine, experiential manner. In the process, he offered new impulses to an oratorio genre quickly growing in popularity by appropriating the musical language of his day for a distinctly spiritual experience.

Mendelssohn's subsequent publication of church music, his op. 39, develops his ideals of communicating spiritual meaning through musical experiences even further, and they might be the best examples of his Romantic concept of church music. Inspired by his regular attendance at Trinità dei Monti in Rome, they reflect his worship experience. I have shown elsewhere that his three motets offer a liturgical narrative from Advent to Easter, based on carefully and strategically chosen liturgical and biblical texts.[38] Yet the motets stand on their own as music for edification. As with *Paulus*, Mendelssohn offers a spiritual experience by employing Romantic musical language and emotionally powerful scenes.

Mendelssohn's ideals about church music at a larger scale can be found in his five psalms for choir, soloists, and orchestra. Psalm 95, MWV A 16, is a particularly striking example of what Carl Dahlhaus termed "imaginary church music."[39] In my reading of Psalm 95, based on its compositional evolution, Mendelssohn's statement, and contemporaneous reviews, the composer offered a spiritual narrative with quasi-liturgical elements to be experienced by the listener for their edification.[40]

Unlike Winterfeld, whose narrow ideas about Protestant church music centered around a cappella writing with the elaboration of the Lutheran chorale as its highest form,[41] Mendelssohn never made any distinction between sacred music, liturgical music, or church music. To him, all of his music with Christian content was church music. He also assumed that modern church music ought to

---

[37] Abraham Mendelssohn to Felix, dated March 10, 1835; Paul and Carl Mendelssohn-Bartholdy, eds., *Briefe aus den Jahren 1830 bis 1847*, 4th ed. (Leipzig: Hermann Mendelssohn, 1878), 52.

[38] Reichwald, "Mendelssohn and the Catholic Tradition," 48–55.

[39] Carl Dahlhaus, "Mendelssohn und die musikalischen Gattungstraditionen," in *Das Problem Mendelssohn* (Regensburg: Gustav Bosse, 1974), 58.

[40] Siegwart Reichwald, "Lost in Translation: The Case of Felix Mendelssohn's *Psalm 95*," in "Felix Mendelssohn," ed. Carroll L. Gonzo, special issue, *Choral Journal* 49, no. 9 (March 2009): 28–48.

[41] Garratt, Palestrina and the German Romantic Imagination, 97.

be rooted in Romantic aesthetics of his day, making use of all available tools in order to offer the audience an immersive, engaging, and edifying experience. As a member of the Prussian Union Church, Mendelssohn did not see an obvious place, if any, to offer his brand of church music within the context of the 1829 *Agende*. He closed the above-quoted letter to pastor Baur provocatively, "If I were Catholic, I would sit down even tonight and, however it may turn out, start composing the one and only Mass written specifically for liturgical purposes. But I won't do it for now – maybe later, when I'm older."[42]

3 An Inauspicious Start: Music for Christmas 1843

Next Sunday, we will have, for the first time, grand church music, which consists of rather small things, namely an eight-part Psalm by me without orchestra (composed specifically for this occasion), a chorus from Handel's *Messiah*, and three chorales with "trombones, etc." That's the king's edict, which had caused much distress; since all manner of wind instruments are now permissible, I have orchestrated things to my wishes; oboes and others will remain. And so we got even only thus far with great difficulty, and in the end, the much-promised great church music, which keeps getting smaller, has shrunk to one musical number at the beginning of the service, and you've been there long ago. ... How, by the way, the chamber musicians speculate about the new instrumental position, the singers about the ... future compositions, and the clergy about filled churches, and all the greedy scheming about all of this, I'll have to tell you about it over a game of billiards or on a leisurely walk.[43]

Christmas Day 1843 represents the culmination of a new beginning for the Berlin Cathedral and the Prussian Union Church. At the start of the liturgical year, a revised order of service had been instituted on the first Sunday of Advent. David Brodbeck has traced the evolution of the liturgy from the 1829 *Agende* to its revisions in 1843.[44] The primary purpose of the revisions was the elevation of congregational singing and an enriched worship experience through the addition of liturgical music sung by the newly organized Cathedral Choir. Feast days would become major religious (and cultural) events celebrated with large-scale choral works and the use of an orchestra. Christmas Day 1843 was the first feast day with the revised *Agende* and the first service under Mendelssohn's directorship. Yet what the king and clergy saw as major reforms Mendelssohn viewed as minimal progress, and he had already grown tired of all the politics.

---

[42] Felix Mendelssohn to Ernst Friedrich Albert Baur, dated January 12, 1835; *Felix Mendelssohn Bartholdy: Sämtliche Briefe*, vol. 4, 141.

[43] Felix Mendelssohn to Ferdinand David, dated December 19, 1843; *Felix Mendelssohn Bartholdy: Sämtliche Briefe*, vol. 9, ed. Stefan Münnich, Lucian Schiwietz, and Uta Wald (Kassel: Bärenreiter, 2015), 460.

[44] Brodbeck, "A Winter of Discontent," 7–10.

Mendelssohn seemed nevertheless committed to his reforms and determined to get results. His plan was to affect incremental change, as Fanny revealed to Rebecka the day after Christmas:

> For the Domchor Felix set Psalm 2 a cappella; very beautiful, very Gregorian and Sistine-ish. I am curious about what the people might say if they're actually listening. Felix would much rather compose with orchestra, and he has prevailed to have Handel choruses follow the a cappella pieces, just as he was able to introduce solo works at the start of subscription concerts in order to smuggle song into the performances eventually. He does all this very cunningly and cautiously, and I do not doubt that he will achieve everything he wants to accomplish. The moral sway of a prominent figure may even be so great as to reform the biggest Philistines and blockheads.[45]

Mendelssohn planned to slowly win over the king and clergy for his brand of church music. The first step was the introduction of the ever-popular Handel choruses in place of the Gloria Patri. Not only would he thereby "smuggle" instruments into the service, but repertorial works would contribute to the musical edification of the congregants, who would have the opportunity to respond with a chorale accompanied by full orchestra. The Christmas service would open with fifteen minutes of uninterrupted music – before a single word was spoken. Yet, all stakeholders would find something to their liking. The clergy would enjoy the "Sistine-ish" psalm, Mendelssohn was able to perform church music with orchestra, and the king saw the elevation of congregational song. The other musical elements for feast days would further enhance the worship experience. The Gradual Verse, specific to the occasion, was again "Sistine-ish" and thereby uncontroversial. The partial performance of his *Te Deum,* commissioned previously by the king, would seem the exclamation point to a service that covered all the bases.

The Christmas service was indeed the major event many had hoped for. The *Allgemeine musikalische Zeitung* took note of the innovative elements while also questioning the broad stylistic approach:

> The Berlin Cathedral has since Christmas a new order in their worship services. On the first day of Christmas, the service began with an a cappella Psalm, composed by Mendelssohn-Bartholdy and sung by the newly organized cathedral choir. This was followed by a gripping performance of the chorus from Handel's *Messiah,* "Uns ist ein Kind geboren," etc., with full orchestra (part of the royal orchestra was hired with pay for this service). Then came congregational singing, accompanied by organ and instruments. Besides the liturgical music and responses, the congregation and choir sang

---

[45] Fanny Hensel to Rebecka Dirichlet, December 26, 1843; quoted in Sebastian Hensel, *Die Familie Mendelssohn*, vol. 2 (Berlin: Behr's, 1886), 275.

CHOIR

Psalm 2 "Warum toben die Heiden," MWV B 41
"Denn es ist uns ein Kind geboren" from *Messiah*, HWV 56 (in place of the Lesser Doxology)

CONGREGATION

"Vom Himmel hoch," MWV A 22

CLERGY

Opening Prayers and Confession of Sins

CHOIR AND CONGREGATION

Kyrie (from 1829 *Agende*)

CLERGY

Absolution (from 1929 *Agende*, specified for Christmas Day)

CHOIR AND CONGREGATION

Amen

CHOIR

Ehre sei Gott in der Höhe. Und Frieden auf Erden, und den Menschen ein Wohlgefallen. Amen.

CONGREGATION

"Allein Gott in der Höh sei Ehr," MWV A 21

CLERGY

Der Herr sei mit euch.

CONGREGATION

Und mit deinem Geiste

CLERGY

Prayer before the Epistle (from 1929 *Agende*, specified for Christmas Day)

CLERGY AND CONGREGATION

Amen.

CLERGY

Epistle

CHOIR

[Verse – Alleluia (Gradual)] Weihnachten "Frohlocket, ihr Völker," MWV B 42

CLERGY

Gospel

CHOIR AND CONGREGATION

Ehre sei dir, Herr

CLERGY

Creed

CHOIR AND CONGREGATION

Amen

CLERGY

Sermon

CLERGY

Verse (Offertory)
Erhebet eure Herzen.

CHOIR AND CONGREGATION

Wir erheben sie dem Herrn, unserm Gotte.

CLERGY

Lasse tuns daken dem Herrn, unserm Gotte.

CHOIR AND CONGREGATION

Recht und würdig ist es

CLERGY

Preface

Example 1 Order of Service for Christmas Day 1843 (with special feast day music in bold).

CLERGY AND CONGREGATION
    Amen.
CLERGY
    Our Father
CHOIR AND CONGREGATION
    Amen
    "Herr Gott, dich loben wir," MWV A 20 (excerpt)
CLERGY
    Blessing
CLERGY AND CONGREGATION
    Amen.

Example 1 (cont.)

after the sermon "Herr Gott, dich loben wir" and closed the service with the Amen. As edifying as this order of service was, the musical portions seem fragmented ("zerstückelt"). One might hope that in the future – as is the case with music in worship services in Leipzig – complete and shorter vocal pieces will be performed, as there is no shortage of motets, Psalms, and other church music by Joh. Seb. Bach, Händel, and others.[46]

Fascinatingly, the writer has yet different views from the king, clergy, and Mendelssohn. His reference to Leipzig and its Lutheran tradition is especially noteworthy. Presumably, all stakeholders realized the uphill battle they were facing. One of the main obstacles was the service's fragmented nature, with everything from the outdated, simple four-part settings of the *Agende* and Handel choruses to newly composed eight-part works that challenged singers and congregations alike. Despite Mendelssohn's diligent planning, there is an apparent, unavoidable clash between the special music for Christmas Day and the elementary, four-part settings used for regular worship services. Mendelssohn surely was aware of the issues – as the king and clergy must have been. Presumably, everybody thought that the others would eventually fall in line. While the service was an inconspicuous start, there is much to be gleaned about Mendelssohn's reform ideas.

Before we dissect Mendelssohn's selections and compositions, it is important to note what was not part of the service: Mendelssohn's initial setting of Psalm 2, MWV B 35 (Figure 1). In preparation for the Advent season and the beginning of the liturgical year, pastor Friedrich Ehrenberg had sent Mendelssohn two lists of twenty-one psalms for church festivals from Advent Sunday through the first Sunday in Lent. On November 13, 1843, Mendelssohn composed four-part settings for seven psalms. Initially, he consulted four-part psalm settings from a metrical Lobwasser Psalter, published in Leipzig in 1584. Rejecting the

---

[46] *Allgemeine musikalische Zeitung*, January 5, 1844 (Leipzig: Breitkopf und Härtel, 1844), 79.

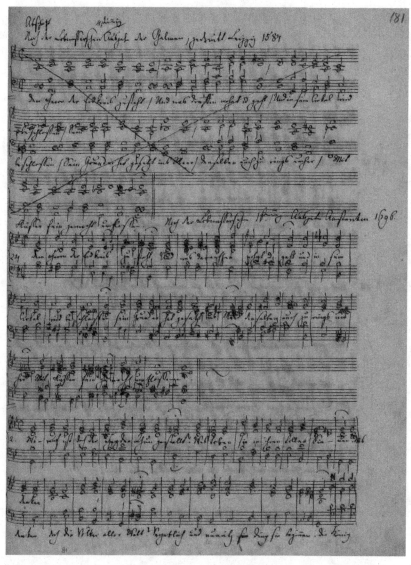

Figure 1 Felix Mendelssohn, Psalm 2 "Worauf ist doch der Heiden Tun gestellt," MWV B 35.[47]

modal settings presumably as unsuitable for use in a "modern" church service, Mendelssohn instead chose the tunes from a 1684 Amsterdam edition of the Lobwasser psalms and provided his own four-part harmonization.[48] For that

---

[47] Felix Mendelssohn, Psalm 2 "Worauf ist doch der Heiden Tun gestellt," MWV B 35, autograph score, 1843, Biblioteka Jagiellonska Kraków, *Mus. ms. autogr. Mendelssohn* 38/2, 181–182.

[48] Pietro Zappalà, preface to *Neun Psalmen und Cantique*, by Felix Mendelssohn (Stuttgart: Carus, 1996), 4.

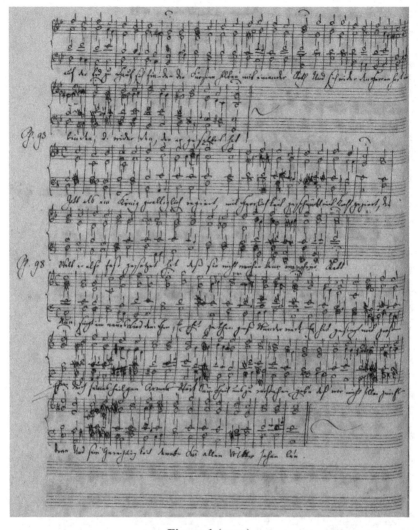

Figure 1 (cont.)

purpose, he adapted the Dorian melody to G minor. Consulting one of the earliest German translations, the Geneva Psalter speaks to Mendelssohn's knowledge of the Reformed tradition and his desire to continue within that tradition. The use of the Lobwasser psalm would have alleviated the contrast between the simple musical liturgy and the psalm. While the Lobwasser settings might have been the perfect complement to the musical supplement of the 1829 *Agende*, they did not fit Mendelssohn's mold of modern church music. The first of the Lobwasser settings, Psalm 24 "Dem Herrn der Erdkreis zusteht," was nevertheless performed on December 3, 1843.

For Christmas, a feast day, Mendelssohn chose a completely different, contemporary musical language with a much higher artistic level and degree of difficulty. Having heard the Cathedral Choir upon his arrival in Berlin, he must have seen their rapid development as an ensemble. Psalm 2, MWV B 41, is a model of flawless text declamation. Its clarity is further strengthened by Mendelssohn's antiphonal texture, which highlights the psalm text's parallelism. Underneath the "Palestrina veneer," however, lies a syntactical design and exegetical narrative that betrays its Romantic roots. Its Bachian influence can be found in the music's purpose to sermonize the text rather than just presenting it. True church music is not just "mere accompaniment, subordinate to the sacred functions, co-operating with the wax candles and the incense, etc."[49] Conceived in eight parts, Mendelssohn offers a dramatized psalm setting that moves from G minor (part 1) through E-flat major (part 2) and C minor (part 3) to G major (part 4). As Larry Todd has pointed out, Mendelssohn had used the same harmonic structure of descending thirds in his large-scale settings of Palms 42

Part 1 (mm. 1–39): G Minor
Warum toben die Heiden,
Why rage fiercely the heathen,
    und die Leute reden so vergeblich?
    and the people mediate a vain thing?
Die Könige im Lande lehnen sich auf,
The kings of the earth they set themselves up,
    und die Herrn ratschlagen miteinander
    and the rulers counsel take together
    wider den Herrn und seinen Gesalbten:
    against the Lord, and against his anointed.
„Lasst uns zerreißen ihre Bande,
"Now let us break their bands asunder,
    und von uns werfen ihre Seile!"
    and cast away their cords from us!"
Aber der im Himmel wohnet, lachet ihrer,
He that sitteth in the heav'ns shall laugh them to scorn,
    und der Herr spottet ihrer.
    and the Lord shall deride them.
Er wird einst mit ihnen reden in seinem Zorn,
In wrath he shall speak to them,
    und mit seinem Grimm wird er sie schrecken:
    and shall vex them in his sore displeasure.

Example 2 Mendelssohn's Structural Design of Psalm 2 MWV B 41.

---

[49] Felix Mendelssohn to Ernst Friedrich Albert Baur, dated January 12, 1835; *Felix Mendelssohn Bartholdy: Sämtliche Briefe*, vol. 4, 141.

Part 2 (mm. 40–63): E-flat Major – C Minor

„Aber ich habe meinen König eingesetzt
"Yet have I set my King on Zion's holy hill,
      auf meinem heiligen Berge Zion."
      yea, on my holy hill of Zion."
Ich will von einer solchen Weise predigen,
I will declare the law whereof the Lord hath said,
      dass der Herr zu mir gesagt hat:
      as the Lord hath said unto me:

„Du bist mein Sohn, heute hab' ich dich gezeuget;
"Thou art my Son, thee this day have I begotten.
heische von mir, so will ich dir die Heiden zum Erbe geben,
Ask thou of me, and I shall give the heathen for thine inheritance,
und der Welt Ende zum Eigentum.
utmost parts for thy possession.

Part 3 (mm. 63–117): C Minor

||:Du sollst sie mit eisernem Szepter zerschlagen,
Thou shalt break them in pieces with sceptres of iron,
      wie Töpfe sollst du sie zerbrechen.":||
      like a potter's vessel thou shalt dash them."
[Transition G Minor]
So lasset euch nun weisen, ihr Könige,
O therefore be ye wise, o kings,
      und lasset euch züchtigen, ihr Richter auf Erden.
      ye judges of the earth be instructed.
Dienet dem Herrn mit Furcht
Serve ye the Lord with fear,
      und freuet euch mit Zittern!
      rejoice to him with trembling.

Part 4 (mm. 118–142): G Major

Küsset den Sohn,
Kiss ye the Son,
      dass er nicht zürne und ihr umkommet auf dem Wege.
      lest he be angry, and ye perish from the right way.
Küsset den Sohn;
Kiss ye the Son,
      denn sein Zorn wird bald anbrennen.
      for his wrath shall soon rekindle;
Aber wohl allen, die auf ihn trauen.
All who trust in his name are blessed
      [denn sein Zorn wird bald anbrennen.]
      [for his wrath shall soon rekindle.]

Example 2 (cont.)

and 95.[50] He also uses recurring rhythmic and melodic motives to offer the congregation an emotional and spiritual experience.

---

[50] R. Larry Todd, preface to *Der 95. Psalm*, op. 46, MWV A 16, by Felix Mendelssohn (Stuttgart: Carus, 1988), v.

Mendelssohn revised several Domchor compositions a year later. Unless otherwise noted, my analyses will refer to the revised version.[51] Part 1 explores the world's revolt against the Lord and his anointed one through a series of questions that are answered by a God whose control is never in question. Mendelssohn expresses the questions through a rising fifth that extends expressively to a minor sixth (mm. 1–12). Harmonically, Mendelssohn stakes out the motet's overall design: G minor–E-flat major–C minor–G minor. In a triadic G minor descent, Mendelssohn expresses the verbalization of the people's revolt (mm 13–16). God's response in the form of a triadic B-flat descent sounds like benevolent mocking (mm. 17–18), underscored by the rising sixth, which further mocks their questioning (23–25). The verbalized plan, "Laßt uns zerreißen ihre Bande" (mm. 13–16), a descending fifth and major second, turns into an octave and minor second as a warning of God's impending wrath (mm. 30–32 and 33–35). Their obvious correlation is further strengthened through the use of unison and shared rhythmic motives.

In part 2, Mendelssohn takes the listener into a different sound world. God's direct speech is initially expressed by two sets of soloists with tight scoring – much like Jesus's words to Paul in the conversion scene from *St. Paul*, MWV A 14 ("Saul, was verfolgst du mich,"). Mendelssohn would use a similar scoring for God's comforting words to Elijah from his second oratorio ("Hebe deine Augen auf"). At the psalm's theological central moment ("Du bist mein Sohn"), the full choir proclaims the Christological reading of the psalm, finding fulfillment in Jesus's birth. Having declared Jesus as king, he is, therefore, also the judge, as is expressed in part 3 in the ever-growing C minor section (mm. 63–103). The transition to part 4 (mm. 104–111) alludes rhythmically to the unison rejection of God (mm. 13–16) and God's response (mm. 30–32 and 33–35), moving the motet back to G minor. The motive of the minor second upper neighbor, introduced in God's warning of his impending wrath (mm. 30–32 and 33–35), crystallizes in the final utterances, "Dienet dem Herrn mit Furcht" and "und freuet euch mit Zittern" (mm. 108–111).

Part 4 offers God's gracious answer of salvation by embracing his son. With the intoning of a chorale-like melody, Mendelssohn sets in motion a drawn-out crescendo in G major, its sound filling the sanctuary until it climaxes at the soaring high Gs toward the end of the motet. Mendelssohn's reading of the psalm emphasizes the call for repentance ("dass er nicht zürne und ihr umkommet auf dem Wege"). The second choir constantly provides a warning with the

---

[51] See website for score.

Example 3 Felix Mendelssohn, Psalm 2, MWV B 41, opening motive.

Example 4 George Frederic Handel, "For Unto Us," from *Messiah*, H. 56, opening motive.

Example 5 Felix Mendelssohn, *Weihnachten*, MWV B 42, opening motive.[52]

unison upper neighbor minor second. This call for repentance is again echoed at the end by the soloists ("die auf ihn trauen").

The choice of G minor/major was not random. Neither was the use of the rising fifth for the opening's series of questions. Mendelssohn knew that "For Unto Us a Child" would immediately follow. Not only is its key G major, but the answer is given in the form of a falling fifth before settling on the third (Examples 4 and 5). The Messianic Psalm 2 is answered by Isaiah's Messianic prophecy (Isaiah 6:7). Mendelssohn clearly tried to make the most of the opportunities he had been given.

The only other chance for any kind of musical discourse within the liturgy is the verse and alleluia between the epistle and gospel readings. Since this verse is part of the feast day liturgy proper, Mendelssohn would have a brief moment to reengage the congregation with the feast day theme. "Frohlocket, ihr Völker," in the key of G major, complements textually and musically Psalm 2 and Isaiah 6:7. The text affirms that the savior has indeed been revealed. All of the motives of rising and falling fifths before settling on the third are the motivic material for this very concise but expressive affirmation (Example 6). Mendelssohn completed his musical sermon before the clergy had their turn.

---

[52] Felix Mendelssohn, *Weihnachten* "Frohlocket, Ihr Völker," ed. Günter Graulich, *Felix Mendelssohn Bartholdy: Sechs Sprüche*, op. 79 (Stuttgart: Carus, 1982).

As part of the 1843 revision to the liturgy, the *Te Deum* would be sung at the end of all feast day services. Mendelssohn's choice to program excerpts from his own chorale setting, *Herr, Gott dich loben wir*, MWV A 20, underscores his willingness to make concessions and requires further explanation. His German *Te Deum* was the first work composed for the new Cathedral Choir. The occasion was a service on August 6, 1843, at the Berlin Cathedral, celebrating the 1,000th anniversary of the founding of the German Reich. The piece was not a labor of love, to say the least:

Dear brother

A thousand thanks for your lovely and kind letter. I almost thought I could respond in person, because I was just about to travel to Germany. Herr von Massow sent me another document about the ongoing saga that made me so angry it almost made me sick; I still cannot get it out of my bones. In my frustration, I wanted to go to Berlin, speak to him in person, and call everything off – but I decided to write, so I am writing to you as well. Instead of getting approval of the proposal, which we agreed upon at our meeting on the 10th, I was given the assignment from Herrn von Massow to immediately write a setting for orchestra and choir for the chorale "Herr, Gott dich loben wir," and it is the longest chorale and most tedious work I have ever done; and the day after its completion, I received a contract, for me to sign, before permission would be asked by the king; once signed by him, the other stakeholders would also sign it. The contract correctly contains all of the agreements from our conference, with six to eight additions in the margins, which negate everything that was the actual reason for the agreements, of with not a syllable was even mentioned at the conference, which will make the whole institute and myself entirely dependent upon Herrn von Küstner, which, in one word, places all of the difficulties of which I had spoken but Herr von Massow denies in the brightest light. Among other things, the request for an orchestra for all church music has to go through the theatre's musical director; for every concert, the administration needs to be asked if the date (which they will set from the beginning of winter onwards) remains or if they will change it, and on and on it goes, with not even a syllable mentioned at the conference. As I said, it almost made me sick. Thinking about your words, it seems best to write straight away to the king and break things off. After mulling it over for two days, I didn't think it to be productive; I, therefore, wrote to Herrn von Massow that I couldn't sign the document and why, and asked him to let me know if the king might approve our agreements. If he did not agree, or if the king or Massow found the additions necessary, I would see the whole thing as impossible to do, and I would have to act accordingly. If agreed, he would know I would be willing to come [to Berlin].[53]

Mendelssohn completed the "most tedious work" within two days. He followed the king's order not to use any other wind instruments besides "trombones,

---

[53] Felix Mendelssohn to his brother Paul, dated July 26, 1843; *Felix Mendelssohn Bartholdy: Sämtliche Briefe*, vol. 9, 347–349.

etc."[54] Five days later, he wrote to Paul that Massow agreed with his objections and that all of the additional suggestions had come from Küstner. Furthermore, the king had consented to discuss the psalm compositions. Given Mendelssohn's frustrations during the composition of "Herr, Gott dich loben wir," it speaks to his willingness to please the king (and other stakeholders). Obviously, he was able to eventually convince the king to allow a variety of brass instruments in church services.

Our snapshot analysis of Mendelssohn's first feast day laid bare the political quagmire of the reform attempts, offered insights into Mendelssohn's church music aesthetics, and uncovered his plan for incremental changes. Tracing the evolution of the two new a cappella works will provide hints about the direction of the reform movement. While the psalm and verse are occasional works written at a specific place in time and for a particular ensemble and purpose, their compositional evolution after their premiere tells a larger story. Both compositions were composed ten days or so before the intended Christmas service to frame the special music for Christmas Day. Having fulfilled their function, it would be understandable for the composer to move on to the next event – which he did initially. A year later, however, in March 1845, he decided to circle back to them. While Mendelssohn habitually revised his works, only compositions of importance were given a second look. Having completed his revisions, Mendelssohn initially offered Bote and Bock MWV 41/42 as Psalm, Gloria, and Verse– actual church music composed for liturgical use. At some point, he changed his mind, presumably realizing its lack of mass appeal. Instead, he separated the pair and grouped his Sprüche and psalms as different oeuvres, making them palatable to church choirs and choral societies beyond their specific liturgical function.

The 1997 Carus publication of Mendelssohn's Three Psalms, op. 78, edited by David Brodbeck, includes the original version, as performed on Christmas Day 1843. Right from the start (Examples 6 and 7), there are substantial revisions. In the original version, the psalm text's parallelism is blurred by the interjections, "Warum" (mm. 3–4) and "vergeblich" (mm. 5–6). Both parallelism and text declamation are easy to hear in the final version. Mendelssohn also moves the first homorhythmic text declamation of both choirs from the middle of the measure to the downbeat, creating more obvious word painting by landing homorhythmically on the word "together" (m. 8). Text declamation is also improved by placing "Herrn" and "Gesalbten" on downbeats rather than the middle of the measure (mm. 9 and 13 in the final version). Mendelssohn then

---

[54] Brodbeck, "A Winter of Discontent," 11.

Example 6 Felix Mendelssohn, Psalm 2, MWV B 41, early version mm. 1–16.[55]

Example 7 Felix Mendelssohn, Psalm 2, MWV B 41, revised version mm. 1–16.

---

[55] Felix Mendelssohn, Psalm 2, MWV B 41, ed. David Brodbeck, *Felix Mendelssohn Bartholdy, Drei Psalmen, op. 78* (Stuttgart: Carus, 1997).

completely changes the unison responsorial phrase, "Laßt uns zerschlagen ihre Bande" (mm. 13–16). The tritone leap (G to C-sharp) would seem an appropriate way to express the heathen's subversive nature. Yet the descending shout of dissent seems more natural, and, more importantly, God's response now matches the triadic descent, "mocking" the heathen's subversive phrase. Furthermore, at the unison settings of "Er wird einst mit ihnen reden in seinem Zorn" and "und mit seinem Grimm wird er sie erschrecken," the upper neighbor half-step that expresses God's anger will turn up again later. By changing the heathen's phrase away from an upward-moving half-step, Mendelssohn clarifies the meaning of this motive. The harmonic language is also tightened up considerably throughout the whole setting of the text "Aber der im Himmel wohnet, lachet ihrer, und der Herr spottet ihrer." Finally, landing on the first syllable on the downbeat of the word "schre-cken" is much more natural.

The square ending of part 2 on the tonic in the original version lacks the imaginative, seamless elision into part 3 with the pedal point. Landing on G major at the beginning of part 2 also foreshadows that the king in part 2 is the son in part 4 (in G major). Mendelssohn substantially changed the harmonic progressions. The first version lacks the drive and clear climax at measure 84.

Part 4 is shortened by five measures. Mendelssohn tightens up the first part considerably while lengthening the final phrase. Most importantly, the ending is much more climactic, reaching the high G one last time as a summation of the whole psalm. The ensuing Gloria Patri is a new addition since the Handel chorus had taken its place during the Christmas service. Interestingly, Mendelssohn offers a more straightforward four-part setting, more in line with the liturgical music from the 1829 *Agende*.

"Frohlocket, ihr Völker" has many minor revisions that tighten things up. There are two substantive changes, however, that deserve our attention (Examples 8 and 9). The cadence in measures 19–20 in the original, which concludes the first alleluia section, is rather square and predictable, as the piece pivots to E minor. In the revised version, Mendelssohn creates an elision with the return of the second half of the verse. Instead of pivoting to E minor, he goes straight back to G major, offering a harmonic solution of the secondary theme, thereby creating a more satisfying listening experience. Toward the end of the verse, in the revised version, Mendelssohn decides to bring back the opening motive, completing the harmonic/thematic resolution – not just for the verse but the musical portion of the feast day music.

Composed and revised at the same time, Psalm 2 and "Frohlocket, ihr Völker" offer a complete, complex, and nuanced and unified worship

Example 8 Felix Mendelssohn, *Weihnachten*, MWV B 42, first version mm. 15–24.[56]

Example 9 Felix Mendelssohn, *Weihnachten*, MWV B 42, revised version mm. 15–23.[57]

experience. Together with Handel's "For Unto Us a Child Is Born," they not only seamlessly integrate into the liturgy as much as possible, but they unify the first part of the service through their musical connections. At the same time, the lack of musical coherence for the rest of the service was glaringly obvious to Mendelssohn. He was nevertheless able to offer his brand of church music, presumably hoping to build on his successes in subsequent liturgies. Mendelssohn had also come to realize the capabilities of the reorganized, now professional Cathedral Choir. Yet it would take him a whole year and Berlin in the rearview mirror to accept the a cappella aesthetics as part of the new worship experience within the Prussian Protestant church. What happened over the next few months set the beginning of the Protestant a cappella movement into motion.

---

[56] Felix Mendelssohn, *Weihnachten* "Frohlocket, ihr Völker," MWV B 42, dated December 15, 1832, premiered December 25, 1843, Biblioteka Jagiellonska Kraków, *Mus. ms. autogr. Mendelssohn* 38/2, 229–231.

[57] Felix Mendelssohn, *Weihnachten* "Frohlocket, ihr Völker," ed. Graulich.

4 Ideals Proposed: Music for New Year's Day 1844

Undeterred by criticism from all sides, Mendelssohn pressed on with his reforms. The music for New Year's Day expands on his vision of modern church music, building on the liturgical ideas proposed at the Christmas Day service. The introductory psalm opens the service, followed by another chorus from Handel's *Messiah* and an orchestral chorale setting for congregational singing. The verse completes the special feast day music, punctuated by another partial performance of his *Te Deum* at the end of the service. Once again, the musical keys of the a cappella works were in line with the Handel chorus.

This time, however, Mendelssohn was not content with composing an a cappella psalm setting. His plan for incremental change had entered its next phase. Once again, Fanny reports:

> Today is the rehearsal of Psalm 98 at the Cathedral, which Felix composed for New Year's Day. Signs and wonders are happening; one can truly witness that the king's efforts to move the church in a new direction are not without blessing, for this coming Sunday, the world will experience that I will rent a bench from the church custodian if I can get one. Otherwise, I will never get to hear Felix's performances because, at Feast Days, the Cathedral is packed that I can't even think to find a spot; and to stand in line for hours, for that I am not strong enough in my faith. I assure you that I will tell you a thousand stories about Felix's deliberations and relationships with the Cathedral's clergy, his deep

CHOIR
      Psalm 98 "Singet dem Herrn ein neues Lied," MWV A 23
      "Hallelujah" Chorus from *Messiah*, HWV 56
CONGREGATION
      "Wachet auf, ruft uns die Stimme" from *Paulus*, MWV A 14

CONGREGATION
      "Allein Gott in der Höh sei Ehr," MWV A 21

CHOIR
[Verse – Alleluia] *Am Neujahrstage* "Herr, Gott, du bist unsre Zuflucht," MWV B 44

CHOIR AND CONGREGATION
      Amen
      "Herr Gott, dich loben wir," MWV A 20 (excerpt)
CLERGY
      Blessing
CLERGY AND CONGREGATION
      Amen.

Example 10 Special Music for New Year's Day 1844.

friendship with count Redern, and their relationship with Herrn von Witzleben; it is a true comedy; we can't stop laughing.[58]

As a bystander, Fanny could find the funny side of all of the political maneuvering. Her joking aside, she clearly saw New Year's Day as a giant step forward, commending the king on his determination to forge ahead – presumably alongside Felix. It is also noteworthy that feast day services had become the hottest ticket in town. Fanny then offered the following description of Psalm 98:

> Meanwhile, the rehearsal at the Cathedral is over; the Psalm is very beautiful, starts a cappella with a solo beer-bass, then instruments enter one after another, as they are named [in the Psalm], harp, trombone, trumpet, and then at the roaring of the sea the whole orchestra, which surges gloriously.[59]

In typical Mendelssohnian fashion, Felix lets the music speak for itself to prove his point. The text of Psalm 98 was the perfect vehicle to plead his case, as it refers to the use of instruments in worship. Mendelssohn could not pass up this opportunity. Like Psalm 2, one week earlier, his Psalm 98 begins a cappella.[60] Unlike Psalm 2, however, the first part (mm. 1–90) is more overtly syntactical, as verses 2 and 3 are set apart as a distinctly new section in the relative minor and a different time signature (mm. 63–90). Surprisingly, maybe even shockingly, harp and brass then begin the psalm's second part in G major (mm. 91–147). His argument is simple: If the psalm text calls for praises with harp, trumpets, and trombones, and since the instruments are readily available, why not make the text come alive? With the entrance of harp and brass, the two choirs begin to lose their independence, singing first responsorially before intoning a two-part canon (mm. 103–117). The following section offers an oratorio-like, dramatic experience, as full orchestra and now mostly four-part choir present a pictorial rendering (mm. 118–147). The vividness of the setting of verses 7 and 8 offers a foretaste of Mendelssohn's *Elijah*. Yet before the final return to D major, the warning, "for he comes to judge the earth," the fortissimo shouts give way to a whispering piano (mm. 138–147). The opening of the psalm's third part, "He will judge the world in righteousness and the peoples with equity," makes use of the psalm's opening motive, which not only serves as a syntactical, structural marker but also offers a straightforward interpretation that God's judgment is right and good, deserving of his people's praise (mm. 148–151). Mendelssohn's Psalm 98 is far removed from the paratactical,

---

[58] Fanny Hensel to Rebecka Dirichlet, December 26, 1843; quoted in Sebastian Hensel, *Die Familie Mendelssohn*, vol. 2, 273–274.

[59] Fanny Hensel to Rebecka Dirichlet, December 26, 1843; quoted in Sebastian Hensel, *Die Familie Mendelssohn*, vol. 2, 274.

[60] See website for score.

Example 11 Felix Mendelssohn, Psalm 98, MWV A 23, opening motive and
Messiah "Hallelujah" motive.

back-to-Palestrina style the king and, in particular, the clergy had in mind. Again,
Mendelssohn uses the harmonic structure of descending thirds (D-h-G-D) as he
did in Psalm 2. The clergy presumably was not appeased by the fact that the
duration of Psalm 98 is actually slightly shorter than Psalm 2.

His sister Fanny clearly appreciated the effort and nuance of Felix's modern
church music:

> Felix's Psalm on New Year's Day, about which I had written you previously,
> was beautifully composed and performed. Yet it was erased by Strauß's sermon,
> which was beyond miserable. One cannot even hope to enjoy this music, for
> while we have the cathedral choir, we apparently cannot have a decent preacher.
> Felix would also have to do the preaching, which cannot also be expected.[61]

Fanny's derogatory remark about the sermon underscores the interpretive
dimension of Mendelssohn's concept of church music. It should not be "mere
accompaniment, subordinate to the sacred functions, co-operating with the wax
candles and the incense, etc."[62]

The "Hallelujah" chorus followed the rousing psalm. Once again, the Handel
chorus had dictated the key, in this case, D major. Mendelssohn might have
consciously or subconsciously based the opening motive on the "Hallelujah"
motive, using its retrograde (Example 11). Regardless, the "Hallelujah" chorus
was the perfect complement. Upon the king's request, Mendelssohn then inserted
his chorale setting, "Wachet auf," from *Paulus* as the congregational response.
And again, the feast day service began with fifteen minutes of uninterrupted
music that included congregational song. By choosing a chorale from
Mendelssohn's *Paulus*, an oratorio chorus, and an oratorio-like psalm setting,
the composer's vision for his first oratorio to turn the concert hall into a church –
which was a reason for the inclusion of chorales – became now a reality. It is easy
to see why Fanny saw this service as a significant step forward.

---

[61] Fanny Hensel to Rebecka Dirichlet, January 9, 1844; quoted in Sebastian Hensel, *Die Familie
Mendelssohn*, vol. 2, 280.

[62] Felix Mendelssohn to Ernst Friedrich Albert Baur, dated January 12, 1835; *Felix Mendelssohn
Bartholdy: Sämtliche Briefe*, vol. 4, 141.

As was the case with the verse for Christmas Day, "Herr Gott, du bist unsre Zuflucht," MWV B 44, was composed at the same time as the psalm. Mendelssohn made interpretative choices that pair these two compositions within the context of the liturgy. Offering a reading of these two liturgical works requires a look at their musical and textual context within the New Year's Day service.

Choir: Psalm 98
 Sing now to God new songs of praise,
 for he does wonders.
 He conquers with hand most mighty
 and with all the strength of his arm

 [Andante lento]
 The Lord makes salvation known to us;
 to the nations he makes known all his righteousness and his justice.
 He remembers his mercy and faithfulness to the house of Israel;
 all the earth's corners have beheld his salvation.

 [Andante con moto]
 Shout to the Lord, all the earth;
 Sing to the Lord with psalt'ry,
 With the trumpet and the shofar
 sing to the Lord, the king of all.
 O sea, roar, and all things that are therein,
 the earth also and all creatures on it.
 O water brooks, clap your hands now,
 and all you mountains be exultant in the Lord,
 for he comes to judge all the nations.

Choir: "Hallelujah Chorus" from *Messiah* (replacing the Gloria Patri)
 Hallelujah: for the Lord God omnipotent reigneth. (Revelation 19:6);
 The kingdom of this world is become the kingdom of our Lord, and of his Christ; and
 he shall reign for ever and ever. (Revelation 11:15);
 King of Kings, and Lord of Lords. (Revelation 19:16)

Choir and congregation: "Wachet auf, ruft uns die Stimme" from Mendelssohn's *St. Paul*
 Awake, cries to us his voice of the watchers high on the battlements, awake, thou city of
 Jerusalem. Prepare, the Bridegroom comes. Arise, and take your lamps. Hallelujah!
 Awake! His kingdom is at hand. Go forth to meet your Lord. (Based on Matthew 21:1)

After the confession [spoken]
 God, give peace in your land, happiness and salvation throughout society; help your
 people and bless your heirs and tend them and exalt them eternally. Lord, bless your
 people, for what you bless, that shall be blessed eternally. May you be praised.

Before the Epistle [spoken]
 Lord, God, heavenly Father! From whom we continually receive goodness, and are
 delivered from all evil; we beseech you, give us through your Spirit these things,
 (also in this new years), to acknowledge in our heart and in true faith, that we might
 be eternally grateful for your mild mercy and kindness, here and there, praise you in
 Jesus Christ, your son, our Lord. Amen

Before the Alleluia [Psalm 90]
 Lord, God, you are our refuge always. Before the mountains appeared, and the
 earth and world were created, you are God, from eternity to eternity. Alleluia.

Example 12 Proper texts for the order of 1844 New Year's Day Service.

Example 13 Felix Mendelssohn, Psalm 98, MWV A 23, opening.

Unlike the texts for Christmas Day, which are a continuous crescendo, the New Year's text starts with praise and then turns inward, ending with supplication and the promise of God offering refuge. Setting aside the valid and challenging questions about German Christian nationalism that seem to be latent in these texts, Mendelssohn offers once more music that expresses the meaning of the text in a nuanced fashion: music that aims to lead the congregation in worship, music that aims to be edifying. The shared motivic building blocks of triadic ascent are found at the openings of Psalm 98 and the verse. Yet their trajectories change. While Psalm 98 continues upward to the octave, expressing praise, the verse settles downward on the fifth, suggesting supplication.[63] The same congregants who offer praises to God are now acknowledging their need for refuge in God (Examples 13 and 14). The comfort in the eternal nature of God (verse, mm. 6–17 and 23–29), expressed through repeated notes, find their parallel in the praise of God's victories (Psalm 98, mm. 13–28). The setting of the words "thou art God eternally" (mm. 18–23 and 30–35) is a motivic elaboration of "refuge evermore" (mm. 3–5). D minor

---

[63] See website for score.

Example 14 Felix Mendelssohn, *Am Neujahrstage*, MWV B 44, opening.

reverts back to D major at the final, hushed "Hallelujah," a "Hallelujah" that has transformed the exhilaration of the Handel chorus into a prayerful acknowledgment of God's eternal nature and its implications for the believer.

Mendelssohn seemed to have particular ideas about church music and the direction of the reforms. Where did his ideas come from, and how comprehensive was his philosophy of church music? Despite his significant exposure to Catholic and Anglican church music, Mendelssohn had formed at least some of his views close to home and early in his life at the Dreifaltigkeitskirche, where the theologian Friedrich Schleiermacher had been intimately involved in the day-to-planning of worship. Years earlier, the theologian and pastor had crafted a so-called pasticcio approach similar to what we see in Mendelssohn's first two services at the Berlin Cathedral. According to a 2002 dissertation by Bernhard Schmidt, Schleiermacher carefully planned the liturgies for his feast day services, as evidenced by the printed service bulletins. Schleiermacher would weave together the flow of the service with the use of a variety of repertory choruses. Handel oratorios were some of his preferred sources. Thirty to fifty members of the Berlin Singakademie would augment his mixed choir drawn from the local Realschule. Given the proximity of the Dreifaltigkeitskirche to the Mendelssohns' home and his involvement with the Singakademie, it would seem safe to assume that, as a teenager, he would have participated in these services. And, in fact, Mendelssohn's similar approach at the Berlin Cathedral confirms this assumption.[64]

Friedrich Schleiermacher preached at the Holy Trinity Church from 1809 until he died in 1834. During that time, his already Romantic views of the arts and their relationship to theology shifted demonstrably from a prescriptive Reformed view toward a Lutheran view that gave music an important role in worship.[65] The theologian placed the worship service at the center of the Christian life and viewed it as a cultural and performative/representational event ("Kultus"). His concepts of practicing theology ("praktische Theologie") represented the "crown of theological studies." His direct involvement in the Agendenstreit (Liturgical Dispute, 1822–1834), about a prescribed Prussian liturgy developed by Friedrich Wilhelm III, further motivated Schleiermacher to cultivate a comprehensive approach to the liturgy at the Dreifaltigkeitskirche, which, upon Schleiermacher's urging, had joined the Prussian Union Church at its inception in 1817.[66]

Schleiermacher saw the mental state of bliss ("Seligkeit"), rooted in the salvific work of Christ, as the desired state of Christian consciousness. While daily devotions in the home offer subjective reflection, the worship service provided the opportunity to experience this consciousness within the context of community. Although all worship services achieve this through performative or representational ("darstellende") elements – word and music – the congregation's participatory elements within the Protestant traditions offered, in Schleiermacher's mind, a more holistic experience. The worship service is not meant to affect something; it is merely an interruption of ordinary life, offering the communal experience of bliss ("Seligkeit"). Feast day services, centered around the life of Christ, affect the Christian consciousness in a particular way, as each reminds us of historical events and their salvific meaning. Acceptable additions are important civic events such as, among others, New Year's Day. The goal of feast days is to reach a heightened religious consciousness, which requires an experience enriched by special music. The added musical elements are to explore the meaning of the feast day and take the place of more common elements such as prayers of supplication.[67]

---

[64] Bernhard Schmidt, Lied – Kirchenmusik – Predigt im Festgottesdienst Friedrich Schleiermacher (Berlin, Walter de Gruyter, 2002).

[65] Joyce L. Irwin, "Music for the 'Cultured Despisers' of Religion: Schleiermacher on Singing in the Church and Beyond," in *Sacred Contexts in Secular Music of the Long Nineteenth Century*, ed. Markus Rathey and Effie Papanikolaou (Lanham, MD: Lexington, 2022), 13–30.

[66] Schmidt, Lied – Kirchenmusik – Predigt, 9–25.

[67] Schmidt, Lied – Kirchenmusik – Predigt, 26–38.

Schleiermacher viewed worship services not only as a cultural and performative event ("Kultus") but as something whole and organic, where liturgy, song, prayer, and sermon are all integrated elements, each exploring the topic of the specific feast day. Intentionality is needed to create unity. The organic experience will lead to edification. Schleiermacher goes into great detail about how all these elements function and relate to one another. Music plays a particular role. Since Schleiermacher views art as an activity that is not grounded in German idealism but rather an activity that can be performed and received by anybody, it should have three stages. First, there is outward excitement ("Erregung"), which then leads to inner mindfulness ("Besonnenheit"). Taken together, these two elements lead to the performative or representational act ("Darstellung"), which is received as an artistic experience. The experience, however, is only meaningful if it is structured and measured. According to Schleiermacher, music is about God, the world, and the artist's subjective consciousness. Music cannot express God; it can only create mood and emotion that explore the religious self and its relationship with the eternal. Music does not change a person. Instead, its mindfulness creates spaces for a religious experience or awareness. Schleiermacher sees commonalities between the artistic experience in general and the religious experience of a worship service. Both are performative acts that bring about self-awareness. In both cases, the listener is engaged in a communicative process. In the case of the worship service, music offers moments of thoughtfulness within the larger context and theme of the feast day. Music can and should play an essential role in public worship, particularly at feast days.[68]

As had been the case with most churches in Berlin, music had been in decline at the Dreifaltigkeitskirche during the second half of the eighteenth century. Carl Friedrich Zelter decried the state of affairs, calling for a professor of church music who would oversee all church music in Berlin. His demands did not fall on deaf ears, and in 1809 Zelter was given that post by Friedrich Wilhelm III. For Schleiermacher and the Holy Trinity Church, that meant two qualified church musicians: Johann Carl Friedrich Rex (cantor) and J. F. W Kuhnau (organist). With the decline of church music, congregations turned to school choirs for help. The choir of the local Realschule participated in special services, including feast days. Unfortunately, this arrangement did not improve the quality of the music. For thirteen years, Rex tried unsuccessfully to found a paid church choir. In 1828 the choir of the Realschule was dissolved, and the choir of the Friedrich-Werderschen Gymnasium, under the direction of cantor Kupsch, took over – without marked improvement. Yet despite these failed

---

[68] Schmidt, Lied – Kirchenmusik – Predigt, 38–58.

attempts, Rex and Schleiermacher had been able to offer excellent church music – at least on feast days. The solution was the utilization of the membership of Zelter's Singakademie. Since many members of the Singakademie regularly attended Schleiermacher's church (including the Mendelssohns), Schleiermacher and Rex seemed to have no difficulty recruiting singers. Schmidt assumes a 30–50-member choir would sing on feast days. Even if Mendelssohn did not participate, he would surely have been in attendance at some of these services.

During Rex's time as cantor, Schleiermacher was embroiled in the Agendenstreit and was also part of a six-member commission, working on a new hymnbook for the Prussian Union Church formed in 1817. The hymnbook was published in 1829. Prior to its publication, from 1812/13 to 1828, Schleiermacher printed song sheets ("Liederblätter") for Sunday services, which were offered as a subscription; they could also be bought at the church entrance. More importantly, on feast days, these song sheets also included the texts for the special music.[69] Unfortunately, no titles or composers are listed. However, Schmidt was able to identify many compositions. The most often performed composer was Handel. It is easy to understand why Schleiermacher often included choruses from *Messiah*. Besides its popularity, many choruses with scriptural texts deal with Christ's salvific work, offering a treasure trove for feast days. It is surely no coincidence that Mendelssohn chose two *Messiah* choruses for his first two feast days at the Berlin Cathedral.

Besides Handel choruses, other eighteenth-century composers such as Graun and Fasch (founder of the Singakademie) were frequently included. Mozart, Haydn, and other "operatic" composers were avoided. No Latin texts or Renaissance composers appear to have been incorporated. Yet in a few instances recitatives and solos were part of feast day liturgies, suggesting that Schleiermacher and Rex used cantatas as their models, creating pasticcios that included all elements of the service. Schleiermacher wanted unity, continuity, and organicism that created a performative experience ("Kultus") with the congregation involved as listeners and active participants. Schleiermacher's theology and views on music were put into practice with every detail carefully considered.

Mendelssohn presumably would have loved to incorporate more of Schleiermacher's ideals. At the same time, he was aware of the wishes of the king and clergy and the changing aesthetics toward a restoration of a cappella Renaissance ideals. Christmas and New Year's represented an attempt to present the enticing possibilities of modern church music that incorporated

---

[69] Schmidt, Lied – Kirchenmusik – Predigt, 2.

everything the Berlin music scene had to offer: a professional choir with great potential and a modern orchestra that opened up many possibilities. While the rest of Mendelssohn's tenure seems to indicate a complete rejection of his reform ideas, archival evidence offers a more complex evolution. Psalm 98 continued to be performed for at least the next four years – with orchestra. It would seem that the king might have insisted on using the orchestra, presumably against the clergy's wishes. Yet it is also apparent that the Cathedral Choir would be the centerpiece of the reforms, and a cappella aesthetics as the norm would be nonnegotiable.

5 Ideals Compromised: Music for Epiphany and Lent 1844

Upon the king's wishes, Handel's *Israel in Egypt* will be performed on Palm Sunday under Mendelssohn's direction at the Garnisonkirche. Grand scaffolding will be erected for singers and instrumentalists. The king was actually going to introduce church music to the Protestant church, and Mendelssohn was supposed to conduct this matter, which nevertheless failed because of the clergy's opposition. Mendelssohn-Bartholdy knows well how to subdue any orchestra and tame the unmanageable and most obstreperous musicians, but not even Jupiter's son and *Alkemens* [Hercules], who has a club called a cudgel, would not be able to deal with the clergy.[70]

That just about sums it up. Despite Mendelssohn's valiant efforts, his politicking and plans for incremental change seemed to have gone nowhere. While Mendelssohn had the blessing and broad authority from the king, who clearly seemed to be in his corner, the opposition by the clergy and Grell was fierce and unbending – which is understandable. After all, at the Dreifaltigkeitskirche, Schleiermacher, the pastor, had clearly been in charge of church music. The clergy at the Domkirche would presumably have felt the same. From the perspective of Strauß and Snethlage, Mendelssohn was entering their domain. He was a professional musician; they were the theologians. Grell had different reasons to oppose Mendelssohn. Grell was the person who had helped build the choir, and the Cathedral was his home. He was much more invested than Mendelssohn. Presumably, it also did not help that Mendelssohn was ambivalent about the whole project from the start, as his letter to Devrient months before his arrival in Berlin attests:

And finally, two words about the Berlin affairs. First a thousand thanks that you didn't withhold your opinion, and I only was upset that it was difficult for you [to tell me] that at the end of the letter you pondered if you should send it. The whole matter, I will admit to you, doesn't concern me any longer. If they really want me in Berlin, then I will come, as I have promised; if, however,

---

[70] Signale für die musikalische Welt 14 (April 1944), 106.

they make my position or my life even slightly unpleasant, I will leave after six months and won't return. That they cannot accuse me of inaction, that's proven by nine years of presence here, and the Berliner scold so much that people in Germany don't really believe them. First of all, I don't think that anything will come out of the project with the symphonies. It didn't appear that way. If, against all expectations, it gets implemented, that's up to those who really want it – I have warned and pleaded, and my conditions are constructive. I cannot promise that I would have pity on the orchestra and their esprit de corps – but let's talk about this in person![71]

Mendelssohn actually lasted seven months before he walked away. Two separate but related issues caused a rift that could not be resolved, both having to do with the orchestra. Mendelssohn had been promised two "autonomous" ensembles, a choir and an orchestra. While the Cathedral Choir reorganized into a professional choir entirely dedicated to the Berlin Cathedral, an orchestra was always going to be drawn from the theater orchestra, albeit with the promise that the best musicians would participate on feast days and in special concerts. Not having a dedicated orchestra meant, in the end, no orchestra at all. Mendelssohn was always sitting between two chairs. He was put in charge by the king but had no direct control over anything. He was to plan and compose music for feast days but was dependent on the availability of players. Based on Mendelssohn's response to Devrient, the musicians seemed less than enthusiastic about the whole affair – and the clergy and Grell were adamantly opposed. More importantly, the clergy and Grell wanted a back-to-Palestrina reform with a cappella music. Mendelssohn realized he was fighting an uphill battle and was not invested enough to keep going. In Leipzig, Mendelssohn had established a prospering musical culture. It was much easier, more promising, and much more fulfilling to continue building his legacy there.

With no feast days until Invocavit (the first Sunday in Lent), everybody could go back into their corners, regroup, scheme, and prepare for round two. Except, there would not be a round two, as Mendelssohn threw in the towel on February 14, acquiescing in a letter to the demands for a cappella psalm settings (see Section 6). By the time the above-cited article in the *Musikalische Welt* appeared in April, it seemed public knowledge that Mendelssohn had lost his fight with the clergy, paving the way for the a cappella movement to take hold in the Prussian Union Church. Seen in this context, his performance of the Handel oratorio was more than just a symbolic gesture, signaling that Mendelssohn was still on good terms with the king. An essential part of Mendelssohn's contract was performances of oratorios, for which significant

---

[71] Felix Mendelssohn to his brother Paul, dated July 26, 1843; *Felix Mendelssohn Bartholdy: Sämtliche Briefe*, vol. 9, 330.

renovations at the Garnisonkirche were well underway. The goal was to create a performance space for choir, orchestra, and organ.[72] The Garrison Church had been the birthplace of the Prussian Union Church, with the inaugural service on October 31, 1817. The performance signaled a continued commitment to the ongoing reform efforts. As we will see, Mendelssohn might have left the ring but had not left the building. That would not happen until later in the year – after it was suggested that Mendelssohn might listen to the chanting of the Anglican liturgy at St. Peter's Church and Margaret Chapel while in London.[73] His relationship with Friedrich Wilhelm IV remained intact, and Mendelssohn would compose enough music to lay the foundation for the a cappella style that would become the hallmark of the Restoration movement. In quick succession, Mendelssohn would compose several eight-part a cappella settings for three services: Psalm 100, MWV B 45, and possibly "Heilig, heilig, heilig, ist der Herr Zebaoth," MWV B 47, for the first Sunday after Epiphany and following Sundays; Psalm 43, MWV B 46, and *In der Passionszeit* "Herr, gedenke nicht unsere Übeltaten," MWV B 50, for Invocavit; and Psalm 22, MWV B 51, and *Am Karfreitag* "Um unsrer Sünde Willen," MWV B 52, for Good Friday. His revisions of Psalm 2, MWV B 41, and the verse "Frohlocket ihr Völker," MWV B 42, as well as the verse for New Year's Day, "Herr Gott, du bist unsre Zuflucht," B 44, a year later are further testament to Mendelssohn's continued commitment to the cause.

Table 2 Mendelssohn's music composed and performed during Epiphany and Lent at Trinity Church.[74]

January 7, 1844, first Epiphany Sunday
    Psalm 100, MWV B 45
January 7, 1844, Ordensfest
    Psalm 100, MWV B 45 with the addition of "Heilig, heilig, heilig, ist der Herr Zebaoth," MWV B 47
February 25, 1844, Invocavit
    Psalm 43, MWV B 46, and *In der Passionszeit* "Herr, gedenke nicht unsere Übeltaten," MWV B 50
April 5, 1844, Good Friday
    Psalm 22, MWV B 51, and *Am Karfreitag* "Um unsrer Sünde Willen," MWV B 52

---

[72] Dinglinger, "Mendelssohn – General-Musik-Direktor," 25.

[73] Brodbeck, "A Winter of Discontent," 30.

[74] Klaus Rettinghaus, "Ein 'Lieblingsinstitut' Mendelssohns: Neue Quellen zu Felix Mendelssoh Bartholdys Wirken für den Königlichen Hof-und Domchor zu Berlin," in *Mendelssohn Studien*, vol 16, ed. Hans-Günter Klein and Christoph Schulte (Hannover: Wehrhahn, 2009), 137.

On New Year's Day, the same day Mendelssohn had made his case for modern church music to the broad public with his Psalm 98, Mendelssohn began refining his eight-part a cappella style with the composition of Psalm 100. The shorter psalm text, set for a regular service, makes for a simpler setting. Mendelssohn nevertheless created a three-part composition.[75]

In part 1 (mm. 1–31), each of the three verses is marked by a fermata, emphasizing a seemingly paratactical setting. The chromatic language, however, of the third psalm verse reveals a more complex approach, with a brief tonicization of F major, the key of part 2, as homophony gives way to complex four-part imitative counterpoint with text repetition. The shift in harmonic language and texture reflects the change in tone of verse 3. After the call to praise (verse 1) and service (verse 2), verse 3 turns inward, asking the congregation to recognize one's dependence upon God in awe. It is a perfect example of Schleiermacher's aesthetic of experiencing art and worship through outward excitement, followed by inner mindfulness.[76]

Part 2 (32–63) of Mendelssohn's setting is set apart by key (F major) and texture, shifting from a simple four-part texture to intricate double-choir. The mindfulness, achieved at the end of part 1, frees the congregant to experience a descriptive realization ("darstellende Ausführung"),[77] expressed in verse 4, "Enter his gates with thanksgiving, and his courts with praise! Give thanks to him; bless his name!" The psalm text itself sets the pattern Schleiermacher suggests, and Mendelssohn amplifies it in his musical setting. Reverting to a simpler four-part texture in part 3 (64–84), the psalm is framed with the pronouncement of a blessing. While a simpler text setting than Psalms 2 and 98, Psalm 100 nevertheless engages the congregation on an artistic, emotional, and religious level, putting Schleiermacher's theology into practice.

As Klaus Rettinghaus has shown, Mendelssohn presumably composed a new "Ehre sei dem Vater," MWV B 48, for the annual service at the Schloßkapelle on January 21, celebrating the anniversary of the coronation of Friedrich III in January 1701.[78] Its simple eight-part texture, offering a responsorial text setting, alternating between unison and harmony, and sung *piano* throughout, further integrates Psalm 100 into the liturgy. The Domchor continued this pairing in subsequent services for many years. Two years later, in October 1846, Mendelssohn reused this Gloria Patri for his *deutsche Liturgie*. In that context, no dynamics are included. Another possible composition for this event was the only recently discovered *Heilig*, MWV B 47. While it was rehearsed, it

---

[75]　See website for score.　　[76]　Schmidt, Lied – Kirchenmusik – Predigt, 42–43.

[77]　Schmidt, Lied – Kirchenmusik – Predigt, 44.

[78]　Rettinghaus, "Ein 'Lieblingsinstitut' Mendelssohns," 132.

was never performed.[79] This brief composition is nevertheless another eight-part miniature that showcases Mendelssohn's nuanced approach. In the case of *Heilig*, Mendelssohn does not use a division of two choirs but composes for eight equal, independent parts.

After a month-long hiatus, the next service calling for a more elaborate liturgy was Psalm 43. The psalm's compositional evolution and publication history are somewhat complex and, at times, counterintuitive. The first version, performed by the Cathedral Choir on February 24, was already composed on January 3. The first and most subsequent editions of Mendelssohn's posthumously published op. 78 contain the early version of Psalm 43. This is perplexing since those editions include the revisions for Psalm 2. Only the recent Carus and Bärenreiter editions include both versions of Psalms 2 and 43. And it is presumably not for lack of availability of sources, for Mendelssohn's wife Cécile carefully gathered all available materials. She wrote, for example, to August Neithardt, asking for copies of all of her husband's compositions for the *Domchor* to compare them with the manuscripts in her possession.[80] It can therefore be assumed that both versions of Psalms 2 and 43 were available for publication. Yet the earlier version of Psalm 43 was chosen and is still most commonly performed.

A look at the revisions muddies the water further. Both copies are surprisingly clean, with few changes in the score, revealing two distinct versions. Some of the most apparent differences are found in the first part of this three-part design. The first two psalm verses are set antiphonally, with choir 2 chanting in unison and choir 1 answering homophonically; this happens twice, once for each verse (Examples 15 and 16). Mendelssohn made substantive changes in both choirs. The two unison sections are the same in the original version, underscoring the responsorial structure reflecting the psalm's parallelism. The final version has a new unison chant for verse two. Expressing the meaning of each verse with specific melodic lines is in the foreground. The changes in the homophonic responses do the opposite. The first expresses the desperate plea through a higher scoring, while the responses are more similar in the final version. At the same time, the wider range of the melodic line gives each phrase more shape. In close imitation, the Palestrina-like texture of both choirs moves the first section toward its climax, as the choirs express the pilgrim's goal, reaching God's dwelling place homorhythmically. Here Mendelssohn adds two measures to make the passage more climactic. Rarely does Mendelssohn add measures during his revisions. Usually, he cuts measures

[79] Rettinghaus, "Ein 'Lieblingsinstitut' Mendelssohns," 133.
[80] Rettinghaus, "Ein 'Lieblingsinstitut' Mendelssohns," 135–136.

Example 15 Felix Mendelssohn, Psalm 43, MWV B 46, first version, mm. 1–20.[81]

Example 16 Felix Mendelssohn, Psalm 43, MWV B 46, revised version, mm. 1–20.[82]

---

[81] Felix Mendelssohn, Psalm 43, MWV 46, ed. Brodbeck.
[82] Felix Mendelssohn, Psalm 43, MWV 46, ed. Brodbeck.

to tighten the structure. It is easy to see why the original version was chosen for publication.

The second part (mm. 37–73 in the first version, mm. 37–79 in the revised version), however, reveals the reason for Mendelssohn's surprising decision to make the psalm seemingly less coherent by having two different unison statements rather than repeating ones. Part 2 runs completely parallel to the first section, with the same unison calls followed by the same choral responses. Having two unison melodies not only offers variety but underscores the larger design.

As Larry Todd has pointed out, for all of part 3 Mendelssohn uses extensive self-quotation ("Was betrübst du dich meine Seele"/"Harre auf Gott"). The final verse of Psalm 43 is a textual refrain of sorts, appearing in the middle and at the end of Psalm 42. Mendelssohn clearly made that connection, having set Psalm 42 earlier. Once again, Mendelssohn's Psalm 43 is not a paratactic back-to-Palestrina setting. Instead, he explores the psalm's meaning musically, even across psalms (referring back to Psalm 42). As with Psalm 2, Psalm 43 moves from D minor to D major, offering the congregation a dynamic, edifying experience. Most surprisingly, his revisions do not necessarily focus on liturgical parameters such as better text declamation. On the contrary, his main concern is to write modern church music that expresses the meaning of the text, engages the listener on an intellectual and emotional level, and is integrated into the evangelical Prussian liturgy.

Within the first two weeks or so of January, Mendelssohn had composed four eight-part a cappella works – two substantial psalm settings and two shorter works. The composer employs different compositional and textural approaches, exploring manifold possibilities of eight-part polyphony, uniquely challenging the choir. One would assume it was gratifying for the choir members to have imaginative music composed for them as they entered new territory. Mendelssohn, nevertheless, had not given up entirely on church music with orchestra. Grell's diary indicates that during the second half of January, they also rehearsed Mendelssohn's Psalm 114. While Rettinghaus has not found any references to its performance,[83] Todd suggests it was performed alongside Handel's *Israel in Egypt*.[84] Psalm 114 is no doubt the perfect companion piece. As one of the Hallel psalms, it would have been recited before and after the Passover meal. In fact, Psalm 114, composed in 1839, might very well have been partially inspired by the Handel oratorio. Unlike his other large-scale settings of Psalms 42, 95, and 115, Psalm 114 contains no solo parts but

---

[83] Rettinghaus, "Ein 'Lieblingsinstitut' Mendelssohns," 133.

[84] Todd, *Mendelssohn: A Life in Music*, 469.

extensive eight-part writing. Of course, Handel also employed several double choruses in *Israel in Egypt*.

The programming of *Israel in Egypt* and Psalm 114 amidst the intense struggles with the clergy was more than a fortuitous coincidence. It was another perfect opportunity for Mendelssohn to plead again his "case without words" for modern church music that included a full orchestra. A performance of Psalm 114 runs roughly twelve minutes, the same duration as Psalms 2 and 98. Since Psalm 114 presents a straightforward setting of the biblical text, mostly for eight-part chorus, it could easily be the opening psalm at a feast day. Its performance in a church (Garrison Church) on Palm Sunday would make his pleas all the more persuasive. Unfortunately for Mendelssohn, his second public plea would come too late. During the final weeks of January and the first half of February, heated discussions about the future of the reform movement caused Mendelssohn to remove himself from the situation. Palm Sunday was his last official performance as Director of Prussian Church Music.

The last three compositions for immediate liturgical use at the Domkirche were written for Invocavit (February 25) and Good Friday (April 5). They were composed in mid-February, just as Mendelssohn was forming his decision to submit his resignation. Remarkably, his work did not suffer from his intense and frustrating dealings with the clergy. On the contrary, Mendelssohn continued to refine his stylistic approach to complex and nuanced eight-part a cappella settings as part of the musical reforms within the Prussian Union Church.

The verse *In der Passionszeit* "Herr, gedenke nicht unsrer Übeltaten," MWV B 50, is found in two versions, just like Psalm 43, which was composed for the same service. As with Christmas and New Year's services, Mendelssohn created motivic connections between psalm and verse. Set in the same key (D minor), the opening melodic contour is anchored in the second inversion of the tonic, A-D-F. In the revised version of Psalm 43, the three-note fixation is carried over more clearly into the homophonic responses (see mm. 6–10 and 16–20 of Example 16). It seems plausible that these changes might very well have been triggered by the composition of the verse, written six weeks after Psalm 43. Mendelssohn makes the connection between these two pieces much more obvious by changing the white-note notation to nineteenth-century praxis (Examples 17 and 18). For the first time, Mendelssohn employed solo voices in a verse, adding a level of nuance and sophistication to these miniatures. The second choral response, starting in measure 13, is much more effective as the soprano line rises stepwise over an octave, reaching its high point appropriately at the word "Herrlichkeit" ("majesty"), the only place marked *forte*. In the first version, the soprano began a sixth higher, creating an undulating, unmotivated line. Finally, the concluding Hallelujah offers a more satisfying, grander

Example 17 Felix Mendelssohn, *In der Passionszeit*, MWV B 50, first version.[85]

conclusion to the special music for this service. By staggering the entrances and cresting on a higher note, the drawn-out Hallelujah offers hope and confidence in God's forgiveness – much like the concluding section of Psalm 43. As with Psalm 2 and the related verse, Mendelssohn spent considerable time and effort revising them. Clearly, Mendelssohn not only wanted to offer his best work, but he must have hoped or even expected for these pieces to become part of the new repertoire for the Berlin Cathedral and the Prussian Union Church.

According to David Brodbeck in his preface to the Carus edition of op. 78, "the setting of the Passion Psalm 22 – Mendelssohn's valedictory work at the

---

[85] Felix Mendelssohn, *In der Passionszeit* "Herr, gedenke nicht unsrer Übeltaten," MWV B 50, Biblioteka Jagiellonska Kraków, *Mus. ms. autogr. Mendelssohn 39*, 52–53.

Example 18 Felix Mendelssohn, *In der Passionszeit*, MWV B 50, revised
version.

cathedral – is in every way the most impressive of the three."[86] Having composed eight eight-part settings over the course of nine weeks, Mendelssohn has
reached a new level of mastery in this emerging genre. Psalm 22 and its
corresponding verse were the first of his Domchor composition he considered
for publication. Neither of them was revised, underscoring Mendelssohn's
assuredness. Yet, at that moment, Mendelssohn proposes a division of
labor for future psalms (see Section 6). One wonders if he thought Psalm 22
had reached the limit of what seemed compositionally and artistically possible
within the parameters of the reform movement. Having provided clear models, it

---

[86] David Brodbeck, preface to *Drei Psalmen*, op. 78, by Felix Mendelssohn (Stuttgart: Carus,
1997), viii.

Table 3. Mendelssohn's Structural Design of Psalm 22, MWV 50.

Text	Mus. mat.	Motivic character	Key	mm.
[1] Mein Gott, mein Gott, warum hast du mich verlassen? *My God, why hast thou forsaken me?* Ich heule, aber meine Hilfe ist fern. *Why art thou far from helping me while I cry?* [2] Mein Gott, des Tages rufe ich, so antwortest du nicht; *My God, I cry to thee by day, but yet thou hearest not,* und des Nachts schweige ich auch nicht. *and at night do I take no rest.*	p	solo lament [rising 5th/minor 6th] choral lament [stepwise descent] solo lament choral lament	e	1
[3] Aber du bist heilig, *But thou, Lord, art holy.* der du wohnest unter dem Lobe Israels. *Thou who dwellest in the praises of Israel.* [4] Unsere Väter hofften auf dich, *For our fathers trusted in thee,* und da sie hofften, halfest du ihnen aus. *and as they trusted, thou didst deliver them.* [5] Zu dir schrieen sie, und wurden errettet, *And they cried to thee, and were deliver'd,* sie hofften auf dich und wurden nicht zuschanden.	p'	assurance (solo) choral assurance assurance (duet) choral assurance assurance (quartet) choral assurance	G	22

Table 3. (cont.)

Text	Mus. mat.	Motivic character	Key	mm.
they trusted in thee and were not confounded				
6 Ich aber bin ein Wurm und kein Mensch,	p	solo lament	e	36
But I am a worm, and no man,				
ein Spott der Leute und Verachtung des Volks.		choral lament		
the scorn of men, and of the people despis'd.				
7 Alle, die mich sehen, spotten meiner,		solo lament		
All they that see me laugh and scorn me,				
sperren das Maul auf und schütteln den Kopf:				
shoot out their lip, and they shake the head.				
8 „Er klage es dem Herrn, der helfe ihm aus	s	mocking crowd	b	47
"He trusted in the Lord, that he would send help,		(*turba* choir)		
und errette ihn, hat er Lust zu ihm."		[triadic ascent]		
and deliver him, and delight in him."				
[verses 9–13 were cut]				57
14 Ich bin ausgeschüttet wie Wasser,	n	Christ's suffering		58
I am poured out like the water,		(chromatic ascent)		
alle meine Gebeine haben sich getrennt.				
and my bones they are also all out of joint.				
Mein Herz ist in meinem Leibe				
My heart is within my body				

wie zerschmolzenes Wachs, / *melted like unto wax.*				
15 meine Kräfte sind vertrocknet wie eine Scherbe / *Now my strength is dried up, even like a potsherd,*				
und meine Zunge klebt am Gaumen, / *and to my jaw my tongue it cleaveth,*				
und du legst mich in des Todes Staub. / *me thou hast laid in the dust of death;*	s (I)	agony's climax [highest pitch]	G	67
16 Denn Hunde haben mich umgeben / *for dogs have compassed my dwelling,*		assurance [triadic descent]	e	69
und der Bösen Rotte hat sich um mich gemacht. / *and assemblies of the wicked me have enclos'd,*		Description of surrounding events (antiphonal)		
Sie haben meine Hände und Füße durchgraben. / *my hands and my feet they have pierced with anger.*				
[verse 17 was cut]				
18 Sie teilen meine Kleider unter sich / *They part my garments among them*				
und werfen das Los um mein Gewand. / *and for my vesture they cast lots.*				
19 Aber du, Herr, sei nicht ferne. / *Be not far from me, o Lord, God.*	s	supplication (solo)		83
Meine Stärke, eile mir zu helfen. / *O my strength hasten thee to help me.*		supplication (choral)	E	84
20 Errette meine Seele vom Schwert, / *Deliver thou my soul from the sword,*		supplication (solo)		
meine einsame von den Hunden. / *and my darling from the dog's pow'r.*		supplication (solo)		
21 Hilf mir aus dem Rachen des Löwen		supplication (solo)		

Table 3. (cont.)

Text	Mus. mat.	Motivic character	Key	mm.
Save me from the mouth of the lion, und errete mich von den Einhörnern. *from the horns of the unicorn thou hast heard me.*		supplication (choral) praise (antiphonal)		
22 Ich will deinen Namen predigen meinen Brüdern, *I will declare thy Name to my brethren,* ich will dich in der Gemeinde rühmen. *in the congregation will I praise thee.*		praise (antiphonal) praise (solos)		
23 Rühmet den Herrn, die ihr ihn fürchtet! *O praise the Lord, all ye that fear him.* Es ehre ihn aller Same Jakobs, *And honour him all the seed of Jacob,* und vor ihm scheue sich aller Same Israels, *fear him all ye that are of the seed of Israel.*		praise (antiphonal) praise (antiphonal) praise (antiphonal)		
24 denn er hat nicht verachtet noch verschmäht *For he hath not despised nor abhor'd* das Elend der Armen, *the poor in affliction,* und sein Antlitz nicht vor ihm verborgen, *neither has he hid his face from him,* und da er zu ihm schrie, hörte er es. *but when to him he cried, he heard his voice.*		praise (antiphonal) praise (antiphonal) remembrance (choral) lament transformed to		112
25 Dich will ich preisen in der großen Gemeinde,	p	praise (choral)		117

Thee will I praise, Lord, in the great congregation,
ich will meine Gelübde bezahlen vor denen, die ihm
fürchten.

I will pay all my vows in the sight of them that fear him.

²⁶ Die Elenden sollen essen, dass sie satt werden,

The meek shall eat, they shall be satisfied,

und die nach dem Herrn fragen, werden ihn preisen.

they with their hearts shall praise the Lord,

Euer Herz soll ewiglich leben.

and your heart shall live forever,

²⁷ Es werde gedacht aller Welt Ende,

the ends of the world shall remember

dass sie sich zum Herrn bekehren,

and shall turn to the Lord their maker:

und vor ihm anbeten alle Geschlechter der Heiden.

All the kindreds of the people shall worship before him;

²⁸ Denn der Herr hat ein Reich,

for the earth is the Lord's,

Und er herrscht unter den Heiden.

and he rules over the heathen.

[verses 29–31 were cut]

lament transformed to
praise (solo)   127
promise (choral)
lament transformed to
praise (solo)
lament transformed to
praise (solo)   150
promise (choral)

would be up to others to carry the reforms forward. He clearly did not want to travel this path of resistance and artistic frustrations any further. Good Friday represents an endpoint in Mendelssohn's stylistic exploration of eight-part a cappella settings.

Good Friday is arguably the most important feast day. Schleiermacher's theology of worship views services as performative interruptions of the daily life, partly because they are tied to historical events based on the life of Christ as the redeemer.[87] Good Friday is the culmination of Lent, as Christ's suffering for humankind's sake finds its climax in his crucifixion as the defining redemptive act, taking away the sins of the world. Psalm 22 is not just a psalm of lament; it is the psalm Jesus prayed on the cross when he felt abandoned by God. It comes, therefore, as no surprise that Mendelssohn's setting is the most complex and nuanced of all of his Domchor compositions. It is also the most intense and performative work. Mendelssohn melds paratactical and syntactical strategies with the goal of creating a communal spiritual experience through artistic means. While offering a seemingly simple and straightforward setting of the relatively long text, he nevertheless employs motivic and structural strategies to present his Christological reading of the psalm as a vehicle for worship.

Beginning with a solo tenor voice, marked *Recitative*, he offers elements of a musical enactment: Christ praying Psalm 22 on the cross.[88] Congregants are not only situated there with the choir's simple homophonic response; they are invited to participate in Christ's suffering. They pray Psalm 22 in dialogue with Christ, exploring its meaning for Christ and his followers. The focus of the psalm shifts in verse 3, recalling God's holiness and faithfulness. Mendelssohn's setting moves from E minor to G major and expands the choir to eight parts. The solo voice is first joined by a second tenor voice and then the basses. The climax of the second part, both dynamically and in terms of register, is reached with the pronouncement that those who believed did not perish (mm. 16–35). Back in E minor and a single tenor voice, we return to the cross. The psalm's third section explores the crowd's mocking, for which Mendelssohn employs a *turba* choir (mm. 47–56). Then follows a prolonged pause, indicated by a measure of rest with a fermata (m. 57). The fourth section (mm. 58–83) voices Christ's agony, first in descriptive, physical terms, expressed by a chromatic ascent and a crescendo from *piano* to *fortissimo* (mm. 58–67), followed by a recounting of the cruel setting (mm. 67–83), which is presented with antiphonal unison singing. Section 5, Christ's plea for help, is set in E major (mm. 84–102), indicating a faith built on trust and an

---

[87] Schmidt, Lied – Kirchenmusik – Predigt, 20.   [88] See website for score.

Example 19 Felix Mendelssohn, Psalm 22, MWV B 50, primary motive
(mm. 1–3).

Example 20 Felix Mendelssohn, Psalm 22, MWV B 50, primary motive,
duet, major key (mm 22–23).

Example 21 Felix Mendelssohn, Psalm 22, MWV B 50, primary motive,
quartet, major key (mm. 27–30).

assured expectancy of God's redemptive answer. God is praised even in times of utter despair. The tenor solo lines, representing Christ's voice, have been replaced by whole sections, inviting the congregations to express their faith in God. The rising melodic lines of pleas are answered by descending lines in section 6, representing an unshakable faith marked by praise (mm. 103–125). The moment of voiced praise ("Dich will ich preisen," mm. 117–120) recalls the upper neighbor-tone motive from the beginning, questioning why God has forsaken him (mm. 1–3). The final section returns musically and textually to the beginning, but the tonality remains in E major. In the suffering, God's kingdom has been established.

Nowhere is the structural design and motivic development as complex as in Psalm 22. His opening question, "My God, why hast Thou forsaken me," is the primary motive found throughout the psalm, returning in varied forms and at structurally important places throughout the piece (see Examples 19-25)

Another important motivic idea is the triadic octave ascent. If the primary motive represents Christ's lament turned into faith and hope, the triadic ascent

Example 22 Felix Mendelssohn, Psalm 22, MWV B 50, primary motive expanded to octave (mm. 43–46).

Example 23 Felix Mendelssohn, Psalm 22, MWV B 50, primary motive, octave, major key (mm. 84–85).

Example 24 Felix Mendelssohn, Psalm 22, MWV B 50, primary motive, eight-part, major key (mm. 117–120).

seems to express the external forces. The first triadic ascent is Christ's lament, which focuses on the mocking crowd (Example 23) rather than lament, faith, or hope. All of the events that happen to Jesus by external forces following the description of his agony are antiphonal triadic ascents in minor (mm. 52–54 and mm. 72–77 see Examples 26 and 27). The recapitulatory E major section begins with a triadic ascent, "Be not far from me, o Lord, God," suggesting that no external forces could separate Jesus from God; it only seemed that way. This interpretation is strengthened by the only triadic descent of the piece, in unison, with the words, "und legst mich in des Todes Stau" (and lay me in death's dust) (mm. 67–69 see Example 28), bringing to mind John 10:17–18, "For this reason the Father loves me because I lay down my life that I may take it up again. No

Example 25 Felix Mendelssohn, Psalm 22, MWV B 50, primary motive, octave, major key (mm. 127–129).

Example 26 Felix Mendelssohn, Psalm 22, MWV B 50, secondary motive (mm. 52–54).

Example 27 Felix Mendelssohn, Psalm 22, MWV B 50, secondary motive (mm. 72–77).

one takes it from me, but I lay it down of my own accord. I have authority to lay it down, and I have authority to take it up again."[89]

Structurally, Mendelssohn uses, besides thematic transformation, also harmonic strategies creating three large sections: an exposition of sorts with contrasting keys and motivic ideas (mm. 1–57), a developmental section (mm. 59–83), and a recapitulatory section with a clear resolution from E minor to E major (mm. 84–150). While the form of this movement is still only the form of this movement, setting the psalm text line by line, sonata form elements have become compositional strategies to express the narrative of Psalm 22 through musical means.

Mendelssohn's Psalm 22 is more than a dramatic rendering of the text. It asks the congregation (and, for that matter, the choir) to become active participants

---

[89] John 10:17–18 (English Standard Version).

Example 28 Felix Mendelssohn, Psalm 22, MWV B 50, secondary motive inverted (mm. 67–69).

as they experience Schleiermacher's three-part process of excitement, mindfulness, and response. It is not, however, the simple paratactic, back-to-Palestrina, declamatory rendering the clergy had in mind. The clergy surely also disapproved that Mendelssohn cut nine verses to present his Christological reading – not to mention the motivic connections and the clear harmonic structural design. Psalm 22 is modern, Romantic church music that offers an integral, participatory element of worship. While Mendelssohn might have ceded the use of an orchestra, he did not give up on composing "true church music" for the Prussian liturgy, which seemed impossible to him a few years earlier.

The corresponding verse, *Am Karfreitage* "Um unsrer Sünde willen," MWV B 52, does not offer obvious motivic or harmonic connections to Psalm 22.[90] What stands out is its simplicity: no counterpoint, no nuanced textures, and no text repetition. A less obvious but highly effective element is the expression of the paradox inherent in Christ's redeeming death. At the word "erniedrige" ("lower"), the melody moves up a fourth. In the following phrase, "und ist gehorsam geworden bis zum Tode am Kreuz" ("and was obedient to his death on the cross"), the line now rises chromatically, as was the case in Psalm 22, as he was raised on the cross. Mendelssohn made use a cross motive at the words "Tode am Kreuze." After a rest at the dominant B major chord, sung *piano*, a *forte* B minor chord in high register in the upper voices is followed by a melodic descent to the words "darum hat Gott ihn erhöhe" ("therefore God exalted him"), only to reverse course at the text continues with "und ihm einen Namen gegeben über alle Name" ("and has given him a name above all names"), rising to the highest point right before the word "Name" ("name"). The piece ends with two alleluias; the first rising *forte*, the second descending *piano*. The paradox of overcoming evil, sin, and death through sacrificial love and humbling oneself to the point of is more than hinted at in this setting.

Why did Mendelssohn not provide music for Easter? If we return to Mendelssohn's emotive description of Titian's *Entombment*, and when we read his letters from Rome during Lent and Easter, it becomes clear that Mendelssohn always focused on Christ's suffering rather than Easter. He

---

[90] See website for score.

might also have found it impossible to offer music appropriate to the occasion without the use of instruments. How could he possibly convey the exhilaration, the outward excitement, without woodwinds, brass, timpani, or even strings? Mendelssohn had chosen his departure well.

6 New Ideals Conceptualized: Preparing for Departure

Your Excellence

Allow me to repeat my proposal, which I presented to you yesterday verbally, in written form per your request.

May it please you to ask some of our most excellent German composers, which have proven themselves with works in church style, to compose Psalms for the Cathedral Choir! It is not inaction or lack of enthusiasm that are the cause for my request, rather to the contrary, I believe to aid our cause with this proposal best, as also my own work will further improve if I can share the task with other highly regarded artists, and if in this manner we can learn from and support one another. Moreover, a worthy and truly ecclesiastical composition of the Psalms is too difficult for one person, as complete solutions can only be expected to be solved by joining forces.

If you mention to the below-listed artist in your request that it is the king's intent to enliven the musical part of the service and that they would be in a position to do so, I have no doubt that each will gladly accept the task and will feel honored to do so.

From a musical perspective, the following ought to be noted: That the Psalm setting must use the Lutheran translation without any instrumental accompaniment (a cappella); that the setting is conducive to a worship service; that the work is declamatory, with as few as possible textual repeats and as little as possible figuration, in order for the meaning of the words to be *comprehensible* to the listener and as truthfully interpreted as music is capable of.

The number of voices, with or without soli, is left up to the composer. It might be mentioned that if one or the other gentleman cannot warm up to the given Psalm, another Psalm from a later feast day (after June 2) might be swapped. It would, of course, be desirable if they were to stick with the Psalm to have everything covered until July. It would furthermore be good if the compositions could be submitted by Easter, as this would give ample time for copying and rehearsing.

If Your Excellency is so inclined to fulfill my wishes, I propose the following:

1. Kapellmeister Dr. Louis Spohr in Kassel for the composition of Psalm 47 for Ascension Day (16 May)
2. Musikdirektor Dr. Loewe in Stettin for the composition of Psalm 68 (either complete or according to the clergy only verses 5–10, then verse 12, 15–19, 33–36) for Pentecost (26 and 27 May)

3. Musikdirektor Hauptmann in Leipzig for the composition of Psalm 51 (either complete or according to the clergy only verses 3–7, 11–15, and 19) for the Day of Prayer and Repentance (1 May)
4. Musikdirektor Neithardt for the composition of Psalm 66 (either complete or, according to the clergy, only verses 1–9 and 17–20) for Easter
5. Organist Granzin in Danzig for the composition of Psalm 8 for the Sunday after Pentecost.

All of these gentlemen are to be asked in accordance with the above-suggested conditions.

That nobody will look at the size of the honorarium for consideration, I am reasonably sure of; yet certainly, I would like to see that the service of these artists is not demanded for free. All these things I will leave trustingly in your hands. I am wholeheartedly delighted that my idea, which will surely be to the benefit of art, has resonated with you.

Once again, for the renewed proof of your kindness, thankfully
I am, as always
Your Excellence
humbly

Felix Mendelssohn Bartholdy[91]

The letter was dated February 14, 1844 – the same day Mendelssohn composed the verse "Herr, gedenke nicht unsrer Übeltaten." His plan for establishing psalm repertoire was born out of compositional realities. Mendelssohn could not see himself spending most of his compositional efforts on a cappella psalm settings. He presumably also realized that an orchestra would not be available for the foreseeable future, placing his reform ideals on hold. As a result, he pitched to the king what he considered the best way forward: the establishment of psalm repertoire that would meet the wants and needs of the clergy and musical directors. He also realized that a variety of compositional voices would make for a better repertoire. Had Mendelssohn's ideals been followed, the repertoire would mainly consist of already composed music – excerpts from oratorios and cantatas. Yet the establishment of a cappella psalm singing required new compositions. The variety of composers would provide a rich artistic diversity. Mendelssohn's pragmatic proposal offered a constructive way forward that would lay the foundation for the Protestant a cappella movement.

Personally, his proposal also gave him breathing room and an opportunity to remove himself from the toxic environment by focusing on other projects.

---

[91] Felix Mendelssohn, letter from February 14, 1844, to Friedrich Wilhelm von Redern; *Felix Mendelssohn Bartholdy: Sämtliche Briefe*, vol. 10, 81–83.

From a letter to Sterndale Bennett, written a month earlier, we learn that Mendelssohn had been in negotiations about an extended visit to London.[92] Initially, he had hoped to leave Berlin for London in early spring to serve as the conductor of the Philharmonic's concert season. Mendelssohn realized, however, that he needed to stay through Lent season to make his suggested reforms a reality. Mendelssohn would leave Berlin just three days after Easter.

Apparently, Mendelssohn had arrived at these pragmatic choices not without a fight. The intensity of closed-door meetings and perpetual scheming is evident by the fact that Mendelssohn does not want to disclose any details. To his friend Woldemar Frege in Leipzig, he wrote on January 31, "About the Berlin situation, I'd rather be silent, which is the best thing to do. If at some point the silence was broken, an awful lot could be said, which ought not to be done in writing."[93] The next day, he told Klingemann that the situation could only be explained in person, only "in a conversation that would last require several hours."[94] The same day he ended his letter to David with a humorous summary of important events in Berlin: "Taubert's wife had a baby, Neithardt squabbles with Grell, Grell squabbles with Braun, Ries squabbles with Ganz, Ganz got engaged to Fliess, Clamor von Münchhausen, walks up and down Charlottenstraße – these are the most important musical news of the last three months here in Berlin."[95]

Humor seemed to be the best way for Mendelssohn to deal with his frustrations. On February 8, he included with a receipt and reference to a "leathery cat" (a leather money purse) the following note:

Dear brother,

Since the recent news about the Psalm singing galled you so much, you will be amused to hear that today a counter-order was released in reaction to the lengthy initial order, whereby, for now, nothing changes. Let's keep this under wraps. And since you shouldn't receive such great news for free, I expect you to put 300 fl. into the "leathery cat."[96]

---

[92] Felix Mendelssohn, letter from January 15, 1844, to William Stendale Bennett, *Felix Mendelssohn Bartholdy: Sämtliche Briefe*, vol. 10, 46.

[93] Felix Mendelssohn to Woldemar Frage, dated January 31, 1844; *Felix Mendelssohn Bartholdy: Sämtliche Briefe*, vol. 10, 59.

[94] Felix Mendelssohn to Carl Klingemann, dated February 1, 1844; *Felix Mendelssohn Bartholdy: Sämtliche Briefe*, vol. 10, 63.

[95] Felix Mendelssohn to Ferdinand, dated February 1, 1844; *Felix Mendelssohn Bartholdy: Sämtliche Briefe*, vol. 10, 66.

[96] Felix Mendelssohn to his brother Paul, dated February 8, 1844; *Felix Mendelssohn Bartholdy: Sämtliche Briefe*, vol. 10, 75.

The same day, Mendelssohn asked for a leave of absence from Easter (April 7) until the end of July for his obligations in London and at the Westphalia Music Festival in Zweibrücken.[97] Three days later, on February 11, he requested the psalm texts for Holy Week and Easter. On February 14, while working on his Psalm 22, Mendelssohn sent his above-quoted proposal to the king, bringing to a close the contentious wrangling about the future of psalm singing. The next day he completed the accompanying verse for Good Friday. There is no indication that Mendelssohn had any plans to compose Psalm 66 for Easter. He would not write another liturgical composition for the Domchor for over two years, when he decided to compose two more verses for Ascension Day and Advent: *Am Himmelfahrtstage*, MWV B 55, and *Advent*, MWV B 54. Somehow Mendelssohn's friendly relationship with the king stayed intact. Upon hearing the news that Friedrich Wilhelm IV had survived an assassination attempt, he composed *Denn er hat seinen Engeln*, MWV B 53, an a cappella eight-part setting, performed by the Domchor in September 1844 at the Königsberg Cathedral under the direction of Otto Nicolai, Mendelssohn's eventual successor at the Berlin Cathedral.

It should be no surprise that Louis Spohr was at the top of Mendelssohn's list of psalm composers. Twenty-five years his senior, Spohr's music had been influential in Mendelssohn's development as a composer. Spohr's interest in earlier music and the founding of a Cäcilienverein in Cassel made him the perfect candidate. Spohr and Mendelssohn had gotten to know each other well, and Mendelssohn realized that the composer of oratorios would compose nuanced psalm settings that would contain the psalm's narrative. Furthermore, Spohr had composed Psalms 8, 23, and 80, op. 85, in 1832 for a cappella double chorus and soloists. However, Mendelssohn might not have been aware of them, as he suggested Psalm 8 for Granzin. Unfortunately, we have no newer psalm settings by Spohr, which means that he either was not asked or had turned down the request. Stettin music director Carl Loewe was well known as a singer and composer and had visited the Prussian court numerous times; he also had performed J. S. Bach's *St. Matthew* and *St. John Passions*. Trained as a musician and theologian, he was an obvious choice. As one of Zelter's former students and an oratorio composer, he would be another composer with shared aesthetics. While he would compose six psalms, Psalm 68 was not among them. Moritz Hauptmann was a friend and colleague, working as Kantor of the Thomasschule in Leipzig, where he also taught

[97] Felix Mendelssohn to Johann Albrecht Friedrich Eichhorn, dated February 8, 1844; *Felix Mendelssohn Bartholdy: Sämtliche Briefe*, vol. 10, 77–78.

composition at the newly founded Leipzig Conservatory. A similar approach to psalm settings would be assured. And, of course, Heinrich August Neithardt was the assistant director of the Domchor. One might assume that Mendelssohn felt obligated to include him on his list. Eduard Grell, however, did not make the list, indicating that Mendelssohn either did not let personal relationships cloud his judgment or Neithardt had been not as much of a problem for Mendelssohn as Grell. Ludwig Granzin had been one of the applicants for the post of cantor at the Thomaskirche.

Mendelssohn clearly organized the list according to preference. Besides Grell being left off the list, the suggested assignment dates are secondary to his listing, yet in pragmatic order. Neithardt, for example, is fourth on the list, but his assignment is for Easter, the first psalm setting needed. The compositional parameters are clearly stated, representing the aesthetics of the clergy. At the same time, he tried his best to guarantee compositions of a high artistic level, written by Romantic artists who would compose simple but not simplistic psalm settings. Mendelssohn wanted to affect forward-looking reforms rather than falling into quasi-Catholic, back-to-Palestrina nostalgia. As it so happened, his sister Rebecka had asked how to experience Holy Week liturgy at the Vatican. Mendelssohn's reply is revealing:

> For Holy Week you'd like me to give you a how-to recipe? It's simple enough: you need to go to chapel on Wednesday, Thursday, Friday and listen; you must not, however, let the unspeakable boredom of the horribly recited Psalms scare you off, because the contrast is used to great effect in the Lamentations, Miserere, etc., and you have to purchase a booklet, which you can get everywhere, in order to follow the ceremony, the text of the Psalms and songs. Most [people] listen to the two to three hours without such a booklet – it is beyond me how they can stand it. It would have been impossible for me to go back a second time.[98]

A letter from Bunsen to his wife not only makes it clear that Mendelssohn's proposal was not considered his exit strategy by the king, but that Friedrich William IV was still actively engaged with the reforms:

> Trinitatis [2 June 1944]. – The king expressed his "wish" for me to stay here until Mendelssohn's return (18 August) so that I may get him to implement the king's ideas regarding the Domchor. The king has named him music director of sacred music of the monarchy, and he wants him to hear at the Cathedral true choral music, which means Gregorian with compositions in church style, old and new. Mendelssohn does not know how to get the thing started and also

---

[98] Felix Mendelssohn to his sister Rebecka Dirichlet, dated February 15, 1844; *Felix Mendelssohn Bartholdy: Sämtliche Briefe*, vol. 10, 84.

cannot deal with the personnel. "He should not," says the king, "be bothered by the Berlin blabbering about Catholicising, which must be abhorred."[99]

Four days later, Bunsen offers further insights into his own ideas about the future of Prussian church music:

> Today Dr. Filitz and I have come to an agreement; he will assume the editing of the chorale book according to my parameters under the direction of Winterfeld and Mendelssohn. This book and the hymnbook will appear at the same time. – I am occupied with the plans for a conservatory for sacred music, for which the king gave me free rein. In the meantime, I listen once or twice weekly to eight singers presenting Psalms and melodies and on Friday night at Winterfeld's all compositions that are in his book. Just imagine we have more than twenty great tone poets in Palestrina style, all Protestant, mostly Prussian: all of them forgotten: – they are the old German chorales for four, five, or six voices, very much in the style of "Inni" by Palestrina.[100]

Mendelssohn's four-month hiatus did not slow the reforms in Berlin, and the king was eager to engage the composer further in the process as quickly as possible. Friedrich Wilhelm IV was also aware of the bickering between various factions. Everybody seemed to have opinions and ideas about psalm singing and chanting. As Brodbeck has pointed out, Bunsen's wife took it upon herself to educate Mendelssohn about English liturgy, asking him to attend services at St. Peter's Church and Margaret Chapel – not the type of church music Mendelssohn ever had in mind.[101]

After the latest episode, Mendelssohn was in no hurry to return to Berlin, and the king's aides presumably saw the writing on the wall: Mendelssohn would not enact their reform ideals. Yet his relationship with Friedrich Wilhelm IV not only stayed on friendly terms but continued to be guided by mutual respect and genuine friendship. Mendelssohn's composition of *Denn er hat seinen Engeln* in response to a failed assassination attempt and its subsequent performance at the Königsberg Cathedral under the direction of Otto Nicolai not only speaks volumes about their relationship but also offers a snapshot of where things stood with Mendelssohn and the reform movement. Here is the letter Mendelssohn sent with the score:

Your Majesty

I ask you to allow me, during a time when from all sides from all over the world, happy wishes and blessings about the wonderful sparing of your majesty's life reached you, so I shall add mine, as each like to express their feelings of thanksgiving that has overcome them, I will dare to do it my way. Ever since I heard the news during my travels

---

[99] Nippold, *Christian Carl Josias Freiherr von Bunsen*, vol. 2, 266.

[100] Nippold, *Christian Carl Josias Freiherr von Bunsen*, vol. 2, 266–267.

[101] Brodbeck, "A Winter of Discontent," 30.

to the music festival in Zweibrücken, verses came to me that I couldn't get out of my mind, and as soon as I found some rest, I had to set them to music. Those are the ones I place at your majesty's feet as well wishes. May this expression of my wish have turned out as well as my heart's intentions.[102]

Of course, what came to mind were psalm verses, and the means of expression was an eight-part chorus suited for worship at the Berlin Cathedral – Friedrich Wilhelm IV's preferred musical language. The piece is more than a gesture; it is a heartfelt expression of Mendelssohn's loyalty. It also signals further acceptance of the direction of the musical reforms of the Prussian Union Church. Not only would Mendelssohn incorporate the piece in *Elijah*, but the short psalm is also one of the oratorio's best-known numbers – a testament to Mendelssohn's compositional efforts for an occasional work. Not surprisingly, though, Mendelssohn revised and orchestrated the chorus for *Elijah*.

By the time Otto Nicolai conducted Palm 91 for Friedrich Wilhelm IV at the Königsberg Cathedral, he had been recruited and vetted to be Mendelssohn's successor.[103] As another one of Zelter's students, Nicolai seemed a perfect choice. Furthermore, Nicolai had also spent considerable time in Rome, becoming familiar with "old" church music. It was a fortuitous happenstance that Nicolai, a Königsberg native, would also be at the tercentenary celebration of the university. As with Mendelssohn, it would take a couple more years and intense negotiations before Nicolai accepted the position. Nicolai would have much less impact on the reform movement, as he died soon after his move to Berlin. Of course, Mendelssohn's impact on the reforms did not end with his departure from Berlin. In a letter from October 26, 1844, Mendelssohn acknowledges the reduction of his salary in accordance with his move to Leipzig.[104] He would compose two more verses and *Die deutsche Liturgy* for the Berlin Cathedral.

Two years after his departure from Berlin, in October 1846 Mendelssohn composed the verses *Im Advent* "Lasset uns frohlocken," MWV B 54, and *Am Himmelfahrtstage* "Erhaben, o Herr, über alles Lob," MWV B 55, as well as *Die deutsche Liturgie*, MWV B 57. The two verses complete the liturgical cycle centered around the life of Christ. His German liturgy provides eight-part settings for the ordinary portion of services. All of Mendelssohn's Domchor compositions together provide the majority of music for feast days from Advent to Good Friday. Verse and Psalm 66 for Easter and the psalm for Ascension Day are the only missing pieces. Since the two later composed verses do not have

---

[102] Felix Mendelssohn to Friedrich Wilhelm IV, dated August 15, 1844; *Felix Mendelssohn Bartholdy: Sämtliche Briefe*, vol. 10, 241.

[103] Brodbeck, "A Winter of Discontent," 31.

[104] Felix Mendelssohn to Johann Albrecht Friedrich Eichhorn, dated October 26, 1844; *Felix Mendelssohn Bartholdy: Sämtliche Briefe*, vol. 10, 279.

corresponding psalms or other planned special music such as Handel choruses, Mendelssohn did not have any motivic material to consider. *Im Advent* nevertheless shares the rising fifth and subsequent stepwise ascent to the major sixth with his verse *Weihnachten* – not to mention the same key. As a result, the two back-to-back liturgical verses with similar texts build a pair.

Compositionally, *Im Advent* is easily the least homorhythmic of all six verses; its closely stacked imitative texture makes the text very difficult to understand.[105] Yet its more adventurous eight-part counterpoint offers a welcomed challenge for the presumably steadily improving Domchor. Harmonically, Mendelssohn provides a nuanced reading of the brief text. While the opening line, "Lasset uns frohlocken" ("Let us be joyful"), moves, as expected, to the dominant, the anticipatory stance of the next line, "es nahet der Heiland, den Gott uns verheisset" ("the savior is nearing, whom God has promised"), is broken into to phrases, which take us to B minor and E minor. At the word "Ewigkeit" ("eternity") in the following line, "Der Name des Herrn sei gelobet in Ewigkeit" ("The name of the Lord shall be praised throughout eternity"), we arrive back in G major. Mendelssohn uses a deceptive cadence to expound on this final phrase. *Im Advent* was premiered a few weeks later at the Berlin Cathedral at the beginning of the Advent season.

Am Himmelfahrtstage stands alone without any musical context, as Mendelsohn composed nothing else for Ascension Day.[106] Since he offered his six verses to Bote and Bock for publication just one week after the completion of *Am Himmelfahrtstage*, one wonders if Mendelssohn made an effort to create a set when he composed the final verse. If we were to try to read Mendelssohn's six verses as a cycle, we must consider two orderings. While the most obvious order would be based on the liturgical calendar, Mendelssohn seemed to have offered them to the publisher in a different order (Table 2).

Looking at the succession of keys, Mendelssohn's publication order makes more musical sense. It would nevertheless seem odd to end the set on Good Friday. In his letter to Bote and Bock, he suggested the publication title "Six Verses for eight-part choir, to be sung in a worship service."[107] Calling this collection music for worship indicates that Mendelssohn did not intend the verses to be sung as a set in any specific order, which might be the reason why he withdrew them from publication four weeks later.[108] Compositionally, "Erhaben, o Herr" makes further motivic connections to some of the other

---

[105] See website for score.　　[106] See website for score.

[107] Felix Mendelssohn to Bote and Bock, dated October 17, 1846; *Felix Mendelssohn Bartholdy: Sämtliche Briefe*, vol. 11, ed. Susanne Tomkovič, Christoph Koop, and Janina Müller (Kassel: Bärenreiter, 2016), 404.

[108] Felix Mendelssohn to Bote and Bock, November 1846; *Felix Mendelssohn Bartholdy: Sämtliche Briefe*, vol. 11, 427.

Table 4 Two different orders of Mendelssohn's *Sechs Sprüche*.

Liturgical Calendar	Op. 69 Publication
Im Advent "Lasset uns frohlocken" G major	*Weihnachten* "Frohlocket, ihr Völker" G major
Weihnachten "Frohlocket, ihr Völker" G major	*Am Neujahrstage* "Herr Gott, du bist" D minor
Am Neujahrstage "Herr Gott, du bist" D minor	*Am Himmelfahrtstage* "Erhaben, o Herr" B-flat major
In der Passionszeit "Herr, gedenke nicht" D minor	*In der Passionszeit* "Herr, gedenke nicht" D minor
Am Karfreitag "Um unsrer Sünde willen" E minor	*Im Advent* "Lasset uns frohlocken" MWV G major
Am Himmelfahrtstage "Erhaben, o Herr" B-flat major	*Am Karfreitag* "Um unsrer Sünde willen" E minor

verses, as the rising fifth leading to a major sixth of Advent and Christmas reappears at the opening.[109] Written just a couple of days after the Advent verse, the connections seem even stronger. Harmonically, the last verse is an inversion of sorts of the first verse, as the concept of eternity and God's kingdom is now front and center and thereby receives a complex harmonic treatment. In the end, what we are left with is, indeed, service music, true church music, written for specific occasions, liturgies, and performance ensemble.

The day Mendelssohn finished the *Deutsche Liturgie*, he wrote to his sister Fanny that composing it was difficult, but there was much to like.[110] When Mendelssohn suggested ten years earlier that, if he were Catholic, he would write "the one and only Mass composed specifically for liturgical purposes,"[111] he never imagined that he would be tasked to do just that. Unfortunately, the musical and liturgical parameters were not at all according to his ideals. Mendelssohn nevertheless took the task seriously, offering a mass setting matching the compositional requirements laid out in his letter about psalm

---

[109] See website for score.

[110] Felix Mendelssohn to his sister Fanny Hensel, dated October 28, 1846; *Felix Mendelssohn Bartholdy: Sämtliche Briefe*, vol. 11, 410.

[111] Felix Mendelssohn to Ernst Friedrich Albert Baur, dated January, 12 1835; *Felix Mendelssohn Bartholdy: Sämtliche Briefe*, vol. 4, 141.

compositions. *Die deutsche Liturgie* complements Mendelssohn's six verses and four psalms, providing complete music for four services: Christmas, New Year's, Invocavit, and Good Friday. Of course, the many psalm settings and verses by other composers would eventually offer music for the whole liturgical year. On November 6, 1846, Mendelssohn sent the completed *Deutsche Liturgie* to Count von Redern. It included the Gloria Patri, Kyrie, Gloria, and Sanctus and brief musical responses. While the larger movements were published in *Musica Sacra* and Julius Rietz's Mendelssohn edition, the complete setting was only recently published in 1997 by Carus.

Laura Stokes has offered a detailed stylistic analysis of *Die deutsche Liturgie*, comparing it with settings by Eduard Grell and Wilhelm Taubert and suggesting that "Grell's setting is the most explicitly Palestrina-like in its stylistic choices, while Taubert's could be described as part of the nineteenth-century version of the *alla Palestrina* or 'Sistine Chapel' style, and Mendelssohn's is the most aesthetically and historically wide-ranging."[112] Stokes further suggests that "Mendelssohn's setting was anything but stylistically conservative or reliant on older models; it transforms rather than imitates compositional references to early music. It also constitutes a somewhat personal take on liturgical music, inserted into a tight framework largely derived from the 1829 *Agende*."[113] Building on Stokes' excellent analysis, I will focus on the interpretative qualities, which were also central to his Romantic approach to the psalms and verses.[114]

Die deutsche Liturgie opens with a composition he had written earlier: the Gloria Patri MWV B 48 from January 1844. For the *German Liturgy* Mendelssohn transposed the Gloria Patri down a half-step from F major to E major. Yet he uses the A major key signature, viewing it as the lead-in to the ensuing Kyrie, which is in A major. One significant revision is found at the beginning of the Amen (Examples 29 and 30). While the January 1844 version outlines a dominant seventh chord with the seventh moving downward a half-step, the version in the liturgy avoids the seventh by having tenor 1 landing straight away on the sixth. This is a significant change, making the Amen sound less modern. No recording of *Die deutsche Liturgie* includes this opening movement, yet it provides common motivic material for the other movements. The upward motion of fourth to sixth and then octave of the Gloria Patri is found at the beginning of the Kyrie and the third section of the Gloria ("Denn du allein bist heilig") (see Examples 31-33). The octave leap at the beginning of the second and third phrases of "Ehre sei dem Vater" also becomes an important

---

[112] Stokes, "Music and Cultural Politics," 148.
[113] Stokes, "Music and Cultural Politics," 162.   [114] See website for score.

Example 29 Felix Mendelssohn, "Ehre sei dem Vater," MWV B 48, "Amen" (mm. 29–38).[115]

Example 30 Felix Mendelssohn, *Die deutsche Liturgie*, MWV B 57, "Ehre sei dem Vater" (mm. 29–38).[116]

motivic catalyst for all other movements. Clearly, Mendelssohn treated his mass setting in a cyclical manner.

Harmonically, Mendelssohn uses the E major "Ehre sei dem Vater" as an introductory dominant-preparation for the Kyrie. The ensuing movements create a fascinating large-scale "plagal" motion, constantly vacillating between A major and D major (Table 5). A closer look, however, reveals a much more complex and nuanced harmonic plan across all movements.

The first harmonic surprise happens at the beginning of the Gloria. Expecting bright D major – in contrast with and response to the Kyrie, "Und Frieden auf

---

[115] Felix Mendelssohn, *Die deutsche Liturgie*, MWV B 57, ed. Judith Silber Ballan, *Felix Mendelssohn Bartholdy: Die deutsche Liturgie* (Stuttgart: Carus, 1997).

[116] Felix Mendelssohn, *Die deutsche Liturgie*.

Table 5 Harmonic structure of Felix Mendelssohn, *Die deutsche Liturgie*, MWV B 57.

Movement	Key area
Amen	A major
Ehre sei dem Vater	E major (notated in A major)
Kyrie	A major
Und Frieden of Erden (Gloria)	[D major ➔ A major]
Andante con moto	Dorian on A (A minor) ➔ D major
Allegro	D major
Adagio	C-sharp minor ➔ F-sharp minor
Allegro	B minor ➔ D major ➔A major
Und mit deinem Geiste	D major
Amen, Alleluja, Amen, Amen	A major
Heilig	D major
Amen, Amen	A major

Example 31 Felix Mendelssohn, *Die deutsche Liturgie*, MWV B 57 "Ehre sei dem Vater" (mm. 1–14).[117]

Example 32 Felix Mendelssohn, *Die deutsche Liturgie*, MWV B 57, "Kyrie" (mm. 1–4).[118]

Example 33 Felix Mendelssohn, *Die deutsche Liturgie*, MWV B 57, "Gloria" (mm. 66–72).[119]

Erden" ("And peace on earth") begins in hushed A minor, which then quickly does swell to brilliant D major. Mendelssohn saw the Gloria as a continuation of

---

[117] Felix Mendelssohn, *Die deutsche Liturgie*.   [118] Felix Mendelssohn, *Die deutsche Liturgie*.
[119] Felix Mendelssohn, *Die deutsche Liturgie*.

the Kyrie. Not only does he not "jump" from confession to praise without a connecting thought, but "And peace on earth" does not happen instantaneously; it is a process that the church is engaged in, as the rest of the Gloria conveys. The continual process of experiencing God's peace on earth has been set in motion through Christ as the Lamb of God. Glorious D major gives way to gloomy C-sharp minor at the Adagio, "Der du die Sünden der Welt trägst" ("Who bears the sins of the world"). Once again, however, the result is not instantaneous, as the pronouncement about Christ's holy character is not as much an announcement as it is a process of recognition, expressed through the movement from B minor to A major. The Gloria follows the now familiar trope in Mendelssohn's Domchor compositions from minor to major.

Expressing the spiritual state of becoming rather than being is further expressed musically in the Sanctus. Once again, the movement does not begin in the suggested key of D major. As was the case at the beginning of the Gloria, the movement starts hushed elsewhere (in this case, a G major chord) before moving to D major. The final movement detours through F-sharp minor before ending in D major, never reaching A major. Only the final Amens bring the service to a close in A major. Schleiermacher's earlier discussed concept of the worship service as spiritual experience through the incorporation of artistic means comes to fruition in Mendelssohn's German Liturgy. Intentionality, specificity, and organicism create a performative event ("Kultus") that leads the congregation to experience religious self-awareness within the relationship to the eternal through the artistic (and religious) stages of outward excitement ("Erregung") and inner mindfulness ("Besonnenheit"). Central to Mendelssohn's s performative act "Darstellung") in his *Deutsche Messe* is the salvific work of Christ, which Schleiermacher views as an essential element of the Christian experience.[120] Working within the strict parameters of the reform movement, Mendelssohn offers a Mass setting that allows the congregation to experience a performative, liturgical act based on the life of Christ.

7 Mendelssohn's Lasting Legacy

7.1 The Berlin Cathedral Choir

In 1845, Neithardt became the principal conductor of the Domchor. To broaden his perspective, Neithardt traveled to St. Petersburg and in 1857 to Rome, indicating the obvious influence of the king and his advisors as well. While Winterfeld's more narrow focus on strictly German/Lutheran repertoire was

---

[120] Schmidt, Lied – Kirchenmusik – Predigt, 38–58.

of lesser importance to Neithardt, Winterfeld's emphasis on the creation of new a cappella repertoire in contemporary style became a cornerstone. Under Neithardt's leadership, the choir became one of Europe's premier vocal ensembles with tours to London in 1850 and Stettin, Lübeck, Weimar, and Hamburg in 1856. A review from *The Theatrical Observer* of the Domchor's London appearances exemplifies the Domchor's success far beyond Berlin, calling their performance "the very perfection of choral singing, superior to anything of the kind which has yet been heard in the country, and we believe in any other, with the exception, perhaps, of the performance of the Pope's choristers belonging to the Sistine Chapel in Rome."[121]

Besides providing music for worship services at the Berlin Cathedral, the choir would present devotional services throughout the year. Lowell Mason, the American music educator and advocate for congregational participation in church services, visited three Lent service in 1852, less than ten years since the reorganization of the Berlin Cathedral Choir in 1843. Mason could barely contain his enthusiasm:

> There is no choir of music in Berlin, and perhaps none in the world equal to that of the Dom-Kirche, or Cathedral. This choir is very celebrated; it is the same choir, a part of which gave concerts in London in the summer of 1851. It is said to be even better than the far-famed choir in Rome. We attended three distinct services at the cathedral, and heard the choir each time. It consists of about fifty singers; the treble and the alto parts are sung by boys. It is arranged in double chorus, and the music of the old composers in eight parts, is often performed; so that one may hear Palestrina, Lotti, Durante and others of the Italian school; Bach, Graun and others of the German school, together with the best modern authors. We infer from their collections of music, however, that they confine themselves almost exclusively to the *ecclesiastical style*, for we find their books contain nothing in the manner of Haydn's or Mozart's hymns, motets, or masses, or like other modern orchestral vocal music. The choir is entirely professional – that is, the singers are such by profession; they have learned to sing, and that is their business or calling.[122]

About the liturgical experience, Mason writes that "the various exercises are distributed between the choir, the people, and the minister, so as to hold the attention and keep all employed. Those parts of the service which are performed by the choir, or by the people are *sung*, and the part belonging to the minister *read*," with the choir offering besides motets "short responsive sentences, in

---

[121] "Grand National Concerts," *The Theatrical Observer*, November 2, 1850.
[122] Lowell Mason, *Musical Letters from Abroad* (New York: Mason Brothers, 1854), 105.

harmony parts, or unison, or a plain syllabic chant, with Hallelujahs, Hosannas and Amens."[123] Each service follows a set liturgy:

> The service is entirely liturgic, or is pre-composed, no provision made, that I could perceive, for extemporary performances. Yet the same liturgy is not always used, but there are different liturgies for different occasions. The most interesting service I attended was one for Passion Week, and which was used twice during the week. There was no sermon, or anything in homiletic form, but only devotional exercises, in connection with Scriptural readings. The time occupied was an hour and twenty minutes; and of this I should judge that an hour at least was occupied by the singing exercises of the choir, or congregation, and only about twenty minutes by the readings (prayers and lessons) of the minister; yet the minister stood during the whole service in front of the altar; and the whole congregation stood also during most of the service, the king himself, who was present, setting the example.[124]

Mason then gives us a complete rundown of the liturgy (Figure 2), which offers valuable insights into the chosen repertoire and how each piece fits into the service. There are six works with the composer's name provided. Three of them were written for the Domchor by composers associated with the institution: Felix Mendelssohn, Otto Nicolai, and August Neithardt. The liturgy is loosely based on the 1829 *Agende*,[125] adjusted to the occasion and its purpose as a devotional service. As we know, the opening psalm (Psalm 43 MWV B 46) had been originally composed for Invocavit (the first Sunday in Lent). While we do not know the specific occasion for Nicolai's verse "Die Strafe liegt auf ihm" and Neithardt's "Vater vergieb ihnen," all three compositions were included in volumes 5 and 8 *Musica Sacra*,[126] published by August Neithardt and Emil Naumann respectively, which would become the repository for the Domchor's repertoire – and to which Mason presumably referred as "their books." The three earlier works by Carl Heinrich Graun ("Führwar, er trug unsre Schuld" from *Ein Lämmchen geht und trägt die Schuld*), Palestrina (*Popule meus*), and Johann Eccard (*O Lamm Gottes*) had also been published in volume 5 of *Musica sacra*.

The outcomes of Friedrich Wilhelm IV's liturgical reforms are astounding. In the 1829 *Agende* music was limited to brief four-part responses without artistic expression or liturgical meaning beyond declamatory proclamation. Yet less than ten years later music has become the central element of worship, or in Schleiermacher's words, music offers representational/performative liturgical

---

[123] Mason, *Musical Letters*, 106.   [124] Mason, *Musical Letters*, 107.
[125] See website for document.
[126] [Various Editors], *Musica sacra* (Berlin: Mortiz Westphal; Bote & Bock, 1839–[ca. 1896]).

108   LITURGY.

also. As I think a more definite idea of the service will be acceptable to those who are interested in such things, I will give a detail of the order of exercises on the occasion of which I speak :

1. A very short organ prelude, of perhaps two minutes.
2. Choir—Psalm xliii. (as it is found in the Bible) "Judge me O God, and plead my cause," &c. This beautiful psalm has been set to music in the motette form, by Mendelssohn, expressly for the *Dom-Chor*, and it was admirably sung without accompaniment.
3. Congregation—Hymn. The instant the anthem was concluded, or rather on the chord with which it closed, the organ commenced, in its loud diapasons, a *chorale*, in which all the people (some two thousand in number) without waiting for the organ to play over the tune as with us, immediately joined. One double stanza only was sung, during which the minister came in and took his stand in front of the altar.
4. Minister—Reading a single verse only : "Behold the Lamb of God, which taketh away the sin of the world." (John, i. 29.)
5. Choir—" He was wounded for our transgressions, he was bruised for our iniquities, the chastisement of our peace was upon him, and with his stripes we are healed." (Isa. liii. 5.) This was sung to most beautiful music, in eight vocal parts, composed by Otto Nicolai, of the old Italian school.
6. Minister—"The Lord be with you."
7. Congregation and Choir—" And with thy spirit."
8. Minister—Prayer.
9. Congregation and Choir—" Amen."
10. Minister—Lesson selected from the Gospels, entitled, " Jesus in Gethsemane."
11. Choir—" He hath borne our sins and carried our iniquities." Music by Graun.
12. Congregation—Metrical Hymn.
13. Minister—Lesson selected as before, entitled, "the trial of Jesus."
14. Choir—Micah, vi. 3, 4 ; music in four parts by Palestrina.
15. Congregation—" Holy Lord God," &c., and " Kyrie eleison."
16. Choir—Sentence or short Motette, in a chanting style, having relation to the indignities offered to Christ on his trial.

Figure 2 Lowell Mason, description of 1852 Passion week service.[127]

action ("darstellende Handlung"). Schleiermacher's potpourri approach, which offers an overarching Christological narrative, is also central to these devotional services. While Mendelssohn surely would have wanted "modern"

---

[127] Mason, *Musical Letters*, 108–110.

LITURGY. 109

17. Congregation—Same as 15.

18. Minister—Lesson selected as before, entitled "the crucifixion of Jesus."

19. Choir—Metrical Hymn, beginning "O Lamb of God;" music by Johann Eccard. Most touching, tender, and effective was the pianissimo, yet crescendo and diminuendo performance of this single stanza.

20. Congregation—Metrical hymn, single stanza, sung to the famous old German chorale with which Graun commences his "Tod Jesu."

21. Minister—"And Pilate gave sentence that it should be as they required."

22. Choir—"Father, forgive them, for they know not what they do;" music by A. Neithardt.

23. Congregation—"Lord have mercy (or have pity) upon us."

24. Minister—Luke, xxiii. 39–43, being an account of the malefactors crucified with Jesus.

25. Choir—"To-day shalt thou be with me in Paradise." Music unknown.

26. Congregation—Same as 23.

27. Minister—John, xix. 25–27. The mother of Jesus standing by the cross.

28. Choir—"Woman, behold thy son," and to the disciples, "Behold thy mother!"

29. Congregation—Same as 23.

30. Minister—"Now from the sixth hour there was darkness over all the land until the ninth hour; and about the ninth hour Jesus cried with a loud voice, saying, "Eli, Eli, lama sabacthani!"

31. Choir—"My God, my God, why hast thou forsaken me?" This was sung very softly and tenderly, with appropriate expression, and apparently with deep emotion.

32. Congregation—"Christ, thou Lamb of God, who takest away the sins of the world, have mercy upon us!" The music slow, and in the style of a chorale.

33. Minister—"After this, Jesus knowing that all things were now accomplished, that the Scripture might be fulfilled, saith, I thirst." (John. xix. 23.)

34. Choir—"Mich durstet," (I thirst,) most effectively sung, in the most simple manner possible, to the music—

Figure 2 (cont.)

church music with orchestra and a much wider range of artistic expression, the artistic flow of the liturgy would have pleased him. And, of course, the eight-part a cappella style Mendelssohn began to cultivate is the common

110   LITURGY.

Mich dur - - - - stet.

The alto and tenor may be easily supplied.
35. Congregation—Same as 32.
36. Minister—John, xix. 29, 30, concluding with "he bowed his head and gave up the ghost."
37. Choir—"It is finished!" Music simple, soft, and touching, as before:

Es   ist   voll - bracht!

38. Congregation—Same as 32.
39. Minister—Luke, xxiii. 45, 46.
40. Choir—"Father, into thy hand I commit my spirit."
41. Minister—"And when he had said this, he bowed his head and died."
42. Choir—A single stanza of a metrical hymn, the subject of which was prayer for Christ's presence in the hour of death.
43. Congregation—A stanza in continuation of the previous one by the choir.
44. Minister—Prayer for the king and country.
45. Choir and Congregation—"Amen, Amen, Amen."
46. Minister—The usual benediction. (Minister left.)
47. Choir and Congregation sang a closing stanza.

Thus there were in this service *forty-seven* exercises. If any one should think the detail dull or uninteresting, let him take

Figure 2 (cont.)

denominator. The primary function is the edification of the congregation, as they worship together.

The reforms had a ripple effect far beyond the Berlin Cathedral as others followed Berlin's model of a salaried choir, precipitating the founding of the *Schlosschor* in Schwerin, the *Schlosskirchenchor* in Hannover, and the Salzungen church choir. Church singing societies, already in existence and newly formed, would receive more support from church authorities. Existing *Kantoreien* in Saxony, new choirs in Hesse, Baden, Württemberg, and even parts of Bavaria would become an essential part of Protestant worship.[128] Of equal importance for the restoration of church music in Protestant Germany was the establishment of the a cappella ideal. Once again, Berlin played an essential role in shaping a style steeped in tradition and anchored in German Romanticism. Winterfeld's three-volume set, *Der evangelische Kirchengesang und sein Verhältnis zu Kunst des Tonsatzes*,[129] provides a summation of ideals for a cappella music in the mid-nineteenth century, while August Neithardt and Emil Naumann's volumes 5–14 would provide the repertoire.

7.2 The Liturgy and Its Repertoire

The success of the Domchor not only precipitated the establishment of professional choirs throughout Germany, but new repertoire was commissioned and published. *Musica sacra*'s volumes 8–10 offer a cappella psalms for the whole church year (Table 6). Mendelssohn's plan of providing modern, eight-part a cappella repertoire for the liturgical year was implemented.

Almost all of the thirty-nine psalms were composed for the Domchor and are the direct result of Mendelssohn's proposed reforms regarding the singing of psalms outlined in his letter to the king cited earlier. The list of composers and number of psalms contributed is representative of each person's impact on the psalm repertoire. Of the Berlin composers, Emil Naumann composed twelve psalms, August Neithardt eight, Felix Mendelssohn four, Eduard Grell three, Otto Nicolai two, and Giacomo Meyerbeer and Ferdinand one psalm each. Composers from outside Berlin contributed each one psalm; Ferdinand Hiller (Cologne), Adolph Stahlknecht (Chemnitz), Carl Reinthaler (Bremen), Ernst Friedrich Richter (Leipzig), Ferdinand Schulz, Carl Gottlieb Reissiger (Dresden), David Hermann Engel (Merseburg), Thomas Sander Dupuis (London), Franz Kästner (unknown). The vast majority of psalms are composed for eight-part choir and follows Mendelssohn's model closely. Seven composers were Berlin composers, while eight were active elsewhere, which suggests that the reforms had reached far beyond Berlin.

The editor of these three volumes, Emil Naumann, had studied with Mendelssohn in Leipzig, and Friedrich Wilhelm IV named him Hofkirchen-

---

[128] Georg Feder, "Decline and Restoration," 384–389.

[129] Carl von Winterfeld, *Der evangelische Kirchengesang und sein Verhältnis zu Kunst des Tonsatzes*, 3 vols. (Leipzig: Breitkopf und Härtel, 1843–1847).

Table 6 *Musica sacra*, vols. 8–10, organized according to the church year.

Sunday/Feast Day	Composer	Psalm	Vol.: p.	Vocal parts
1st Advent	August Neithardt	Psalm 24, op. 134	8: 2	SSAATTBB
2nd Advent	Emil Naumann	Psalm 80, op. 20	8: 8	SSAATTBB
3rd Advent	Emil Naumann	Psalm 83, op. 19	8: 19	SATB SATB
4th Advent	Emil Naumann	Psalm 19, op. 17	8: 32	SATB SATB
1st Christmas Day	Felix Mendelssohn	Psalm 2, MWV	8: 39	SATB SATB
2nd Christmas Day	Ferdinand Hiller	Psalm 119, op. 65	8: 56	SATB SATB
Sunday after Christmas	Emil Naumann	Psalm 93, op. 18	8: 73	SSAATTBB
New Year's Day	Franz Kästner	Psalm 98	8: 81	SSAATTBB
Sunday after New Year	August Neithardt	Psalm 72	8: 86	SSAATTBB
1st Sunday after Epiphany	Felix Mendelssohn	Psalm 100, MWV	8: 91	SSAATTBB
2nd Sunday after Epiphany/ Jubilate/Rogate	August Neithardt	Psalm 66, op. 10, no. 2	8: 96	SSAATTBB
3rd–6th Sunday after Epiphany	Otto Nicolai	Psalm 97	8: 102	SATB
Septuagesima/2nd Sunday after Trinitatis	Thomas Sanders Dupuis	Psalm 18 (Psalmody)	9: 110	SATB
Sexagesimae	August Neithardt	Psalm 44	9: 112	SSAATTBB
Estomini	Otto Nicolai	Psalm 31	9: 113	SSAATTBB
Invocavit	Giacomo Meyerbeer	Psalm 91	9: 127	SSAATTBB
Reminiscere/Oculi/3rd Sunday after Trinitatis	Emil Naumann	Psalm 25, op. 15	9: 151	SATB
Laetare/18th and 19th Sunday after Trinitas	Emil Naumann	Psalm 122	9: 156	SSAATTBB
Judica	Felix Mendelssohn	Psalm 43, MWV	9: 164	SSAATTBB
Palm Sunday/Good Friday	Felix Mendelssohn	Psalm 22, MWV	9: 173	SSAATTBB
Maundy Thursday	August Neithardt	Psalm 67	9: 190	SATB SATB

Occasion	Composer	Psalm	Reference	Voicing
Easter Sunday/Easter Monday	Emil Naumann	Psalm 66 (Psalmody)	9: 196	SSATB
Quasimodogeniti/2nd Day of Pentecost	David Hermann Engel	Psalm 81	9: 202	SSAATTBB
Misericordias	Eduard Grell	Psalm 130	9: 208	SATB SATB
Day of Repentance	Eduard Grell	Psalm 51	9: 213	SAATTTBB SATB
Ascension Day	Emil Naumann	Psalm 47, op. 10, no. 1 (Psalmody)	9: 229	SATB SATB
Exaudi/4th and 5th Sunday after Trinitatis	Carl Gottlieb Reissiger	Psalm 27	9: 233	SATB SATB
Pentecost/11th Sunday after Trinitatis	Ferdinand Schulz	Psalm 68, op. 39	9: 247	SATB SATB
Trinitatis	Emil Naumann	Psalm 6	10: 262	SSAATTBB
1st Sunday after Trinitatis	August Neithardt	Psalm 11	10: 267	SSAATTBB
6th Sunday after Trinitatis	Emil Naumann	Psalm 23	10: 274	SATB SATB
7th Sunday after Trinitatis	August Neithardt	Psalm 47, op. 138	10: 278	SAATTBB
8th Sunday after Trinitatis	Ernst Friedrich Richter	Psalm 48	10: 283	SATB SATB
9th Sunday after Trinitatis	August Neithardt	Psalm 54, op. 138	10: 292	SSAATTBB
10th Sunday after Trinitatis	Emil Naumann	Psalm 55	10: 298	SATB
12th Sunday after Trinitatis	Carl Reintaler	Psalm 70	10: 304	SATB SATB
13th Sunday after Trinitatis	Adolph Stahlknecht	Psalm 74, op. 15	10: 315	SATB
14th and 15th Sunday after Trinitatis	Emil Naumann	Psalm 20, op. 11, No. 2	10: 322	SSAATTBB
Sunday in Memory of the Deceased	Eduard Grell	Psalm 90	10: 326	SATB SATB

Musikdirektor in 1856. The dedication and preface of volume 8 offer fascinating insights into the developments over the next ten years after Mendelssohn's departure from Berlin.

> Accept, your royal majesty, humbly with this work, the result of multi-year labor to bring to fruition the royal majesty's idea to introduce the singing of Psalms in the Protestant Church. The editor hopes to have accomplished that nothing ecclesiastical nor musical would stand in the way of completing the beautiful but too often considered impossible task of having the congregation participate in Psalm singing. Of course, the lofty task of developing an alternating psalmody between choir and congregation that reflects the parallelism of Psalm verses could not be solved all at once. If this collection offered a means to move the congregation toward the goal of performing Psalms in alternation with artistic choral presentations, then it has accomplished its task in moving toward that goal, which your royal majesty's enlightened vision has kept in focus without wavering or perceived prejudices for all these many years.[130]

Naumann's dedication is perplexing but sincere. Rather than celebrating the feat of providing a complete set of psalms settings for the church year, Naumann seems to view the anthology as merely a stepping stone toward Friedrich Wilhelm IV's ultimate desire for the congregants to be at the center of psalm singing, where congregational singing is to be the hallmark of Protestant worship. In the long, and at times tedious, preface Naumann explains his aims in greater detail. He recounts the history of Protestant church music, anchored in Luther's love for music and Calvin's insistence on psalm singing. At the same time, Naumann finds important stylistic cues for Protestant worship at the Vatican, Westminster Abbey, churches in Switzerland, and Catholic congregations in Prussian Rhineland. Naumann's vision for Protestant psalmody incorporates an antiphonal recitation between complex choral settings and homophonic singing by a knowledgeable and, to some degree, trained congregation. By recitation, Naumann refers to easily understandable, syllabic text settings, which could, in the case of the choir, consist of complex polyphony; he upholds Mendelssohn's psalms as exemplary. His three volumes of *Musica sacra* include three examples of psalmody. The first, by Dupuis, represents 1760s English psalmody; the other two are Naumann's attempts. Yet he is under no illusion that the king's ideas about antiphonal psalmody are close to becoming a reality.

Within this framework, Naumann does celebrate the accomplishment of publishing artistic psalm settings for the entire church year. Both in variety and quality, the psalms had become the hallmark of the Prussian Protestant

---

[130] *Musica sacra*, vol. 8, ed. Emil Naumann (Berlin: Bote & Bock, 1855), dedication.

church, and the Berlin Cathedral had been and continued to be at the center of liturgical reforms. Mendelssohn's pivotal role is, according to Naumann, undeniable:

> Felix Mendelssohn, in whom Protestant Christendom was lively at work, was appointed to create a form for Psalm singing that, on the one hand, would allow for congregational participation and, on the other hand, would raise artistry to its fullest extent.
>
> Yet the immortalized master was unwilling to ponder congregational participation since it would seem to preclude artistry, and he was unsuspecting that such a form could be found in history, where congregational participation and artistry had become a reality.
>
> We are talking about his for the royal Domchor composed Psalms. Although they offer no place for congregational participation, they fulfill, to a high degree, another demand for the musical performance of Psalms in the Protestant church of no lesser importance. Which is: the emphasis on each word, or musical recitation. . . .
>
> Although we only possess the 2nd, 22nd, 43rd, and 100th Psalms composed in this manner [by Mendelssohn], these nevertheless suffice to demonstrate how much can be done in this manner. The form is wholly built around the Psalm text and its pregnant and concise expression, just the way in which they can only be used in the Protestant service, where the length of the sermon should not be curtailed.
>
> In this manner, he created an entirely new, for Protestant liturgical needs appropriate, art form, which all those who are familiar with these needs appreciate. And one such as this one we were in need of; although we are in no way opposed to the performance of expressly for the worship service composed unsurpassed masterworks by Palestrina, Lotti, Gabrieli, etc. in our churches, we cannot conceal that, apart from the transcription of the biblical word from the original Latin text, which is unavoidable, they also preclude any musical participation from the congregation in song. . . .
>
> Unfortunately, Mendelssohn's for the Psalms created artform, which does not yet allow for congregational participation through singing, was met with stiff resistance by members [of the congregation] and part of the clergy. One could find in them arbitrary innovations, bemoaned the interference with the essential simplicity of the Protestant worship service, etc. Only few recognized straightaway how much this way of composing and performing of Psalms befits the character of Protestant worship services. We are happy to have found among those few first and foremost Count F. W. v. Redern, General Director of Royal Court Music, whose directive it was for the younger composers, who had been asked to provide the still missing Psalms for liturgical use by the royal Domchor, to be given Mendelssohn's compositions as models.[131]

---

[131] *Musica sacra*, vol. 8, preface.

Naumann also refers to Mendelssohn's *Deutsche Liturgie* as one of his models for his own liturgy, which is included in the appendix of volume 10. The three central parts of Mendelssohn's liturgy, his Kyrie, Gloria, and Sanctus, had already been published in volumes 5 (Kyrie) and 7 (Gloria and Sanctus).

It is fascinating how Naumann traces the establishment of the eight-part psalm settings, referencing, in particular, the initial resistance to Mendelssohn's novel settings. Yet Naumann never questions the a cappella aesthetics. As we have already seen in Mason's musical letter, a cappella singing had become the hallmark of the Prussian liturgy. The Cathedral Choir would supplement the psalm settings, verses, and short liturgical responses with mostly sixteenth- and seventeenth-century repertoire, creating performative and narrative services, not unlike those planned by Schleiermacher and Mendelssohn. Prussian liturgy would continue along these patterns, as Naumann's visions of psalmody never materialized. Instead, volumes 11–14 of *Musica sacra* contain more music by "old" masters (Figure 3).

The initial musical reforms at the Berlin Cathedral, precipitated by the formation of the Prussian Union Church, are part of broader developments in church music. While renewed interest in a cappella music during the second half of nineteenth century within the Catholic church brought about the Caecilian movement, things are more complex within the Protestant traditions. Paid choirs such as the Berlin Domchor Berlin, Schlosschor Schwerin, Schlosskirchenchor Hannover, and the Salzungen church choir were only a small part of the genesis of the a cappella movement. Church singing societies that began in the 1870s as part of a lay movement would have an even broader impact, offering more participation with far less cost. With support from church authorities, associations such as the *Evangelischer Kirchengesangsverein für Deutschland* of the *Verband evangelischer Kirchenchöre Deutschlands* church choirs with or without paid singers would contribute in church life in various ways – most notably weekly participation in the liturgy.[132]

When Mendelssohn became Director of Prussian Church Music, he assumed that he would establish a distinct, new brand of modern church music. Drawing on his experiences in Berlin under Schleiermacher and his travels to the Vatican, Mendelssohn hoped to offer an edifying worship experience where choir, soloists, and orchestra would become an indispensable part of the liturgy, which he saw as a performative act, centered primarily around the life of Christ. Yet he quickly realized that the court and clergy were not interested in his foundational concepts of true church music; they merely wanted reforms, based on the restauration ideals espoused by Winterfeld and Thibaut.

---

[132] Feder, "Decline and Restoration," 383–385.

Figure 3 Table of contents in *Musica sacra* 9, listing volumes 1–14.[133]

Outnumbered by the clergy and musical staff at the Berlin Cathedral, he begrudgingly accepted the limitations of a cappella singing and the music's limited scope in the liturgy. Having previously composed eight-part works such as *Mitten wir im Leben sind*, MWV B 21, he cultivated a complex and nuanced a cappella style that placed the interpretation of the psalm text at its center. Mendelssohn strove to engage the listener in worship by offering an edifying, experiential presentation of the text. With the composition of *Die deutsche Liturgie*, Mendelssohn completed music five liturgies from Advent to Good

---

[133] *Musica sacra*, vol. 9, ed. Emil Naumann (Berlin: Bote & Bock, 1855).

Figure 3 (cont.)

Friday. His eight-part compositional style became the model for dozens of contemporaneous psalm settings. Beyond its immediate impact, his a cappella aesthetics more broadly influenced sacred music in the Protestant tradition, culminating in repertorial sacred works by Brahms, Hugo Distler, and Ernst Pepping.

Bibliography

Agende für die Evangelische Kirche in den KöniglichPreußischen Landen. Berlin: Dietericischen Buchdruckerei, 1829.

Allgemeine musikalische Zeitung, January 5, 1844. Leipzig: Breitkopf und Härtel, 1844.

Brodbeck, David. "A Winter of Discontent: Mendelssohn and the *Berliner Domchor.*" In *Mendelssohn Studies*, edited by R. Larry Todd, 1–32. Cambridge: Cambridge University Press, 1992.

"Brahms's Mendelssohn." In *Brahms Studies*, vol. 2, edited by David Brodbeck, 209–231. Lincoln, NE: University of Nebraska Press, 1998.

Carlson, Julius Reder. "Politics without Words: Mendelssohn and His Music in Restoration-Era Prussia (1841–47)." PhD diss. University of California–Los Angeles, 2015.

Clark, Christopher. *Iron Kingdom: The Rise and Downfall of Prussia, 1600–1947.* Cambridge, MA: Harvard University Press, 2006.

Dahlhaus, Carl. "Mendelssohn und die musikalischen Gattungstraditionen." In *Das Problem Mendelssohn*, 55–60, edited by Carl Dahlhaus, Regensburg: Gustav Bosse, 1974.

Dinglinger, Wolfgang. "Mendelssohn: General-Musik-Direktor für kirchliche und geistliche Musik." In *Felix Mendelssohn Bartholdy: Kongreß-Bericht Berlin 1994*, edited by Christian Martin Schmidt, 23–37. Wiesbaden: Breitkopf & Härtel, 1997.

Feder, Georg. "Decline and Restoration." Translated by Reinhard G. Pauly. In *Protestant Church Music*, edited by Friedrich Blume, 317–404. New York: W. W. Norton, 1974.

Garratt, James. *Palestrina and the German Romantic Imagination: Interpreting Historicism in Nineteenth-Century Music.* Cambridge: Cambridge University Press, 2002.

Hensel, Sebastian. *Die Familie Mendelssohn.* 2 vols. Berlin: Behr's, 1886.

Irwin, Joyce L. "Music for the 'Cultured Despisers' of Religion: Schleiermacher on Singing in the Church and Beyond." In *Sacred Contexts in Secular Music of the Long Nineteenth Century*, edited by Markus Rathey and Effie Papanikolaou, 13–30. Lanham, MD: Lexington, 2022.

Liturgie zum Hauptgottesdienste an Sonn- und Festtagen und zur Abendsmahlfeier für die evangelische Kirche des Preußischen Staats. Berlin: Wilhelm Dieterici, 1823.

Loos, Helmut and Wilhelm Seider. *Felix Mendelssohn Bartholdy: Sämtliche Briefe.* 12 vols. Kassel: Bärenreiter, 2008–2017.

Mason, Lowell. *Musical Letters from Abroad.* New York: Mason Brothers, 1854.

Mendelssohn, Felix. *Der 95. Psalm*, op. 46. Edited by R. Larry Todd. Stuttgart: Carus, 1988.

Felix Mendelssohn: Die deutsche Liturgie, MWV B 57. Edited by Judith Silber Ballan. Stuttgart: Carus, 1997.

Felix Mendelssohn Bartholdy, Drei Psalmen, op. 78. Edited by David Brodbeck. Stuttgart: Carus, 1997.

Felix Mendelssohn Bartholody, Psalmen, op. 78. Edited by John Michael Cooper. Kassel: Bärenreiter, 2006.

Felix Mendelssohn Bartholdy: Sechs Sprüche, op. 79. Edited by Günter Graulich. Stuttgart: Carus, 1982.

Neun Psalmen und Cantique. Edited by Pietro Zappalà. Stuttgart: Carus, 1996.

Nippold, Friedrich, *Christian Carl Josias Freiherr von Bunsen: Aus Briefen und nach eigener Erinnerung geschildert.* Vol 2. Leipzig: Brockhaus, 1869.

Reichwald, Siegwart. "Lost in Translation: The Case of Felix Mendelssohn's *Psalm 95.*" In "Felix Mendelssohn," edited by Carroll L. Gonzo, special issue. *Choral Journal* 49, no. 9 (March 2009): 28–48.

"Mendelssohn and the Catholic Tradition: Roman Influences on His Kirchen-Musik, Op. 23 and Drei Motetten, Op. 39." In *Mendelssohn, the Organ, and the Music of the Past*, edited by Jürgen Thym, 40–60. Rochester, NY: University of Rochester Press, 2014.

Rettinghaus, Klaus. "Ein 'Lieblingsinstitut' Mendelssohns: Neue Quellen zu Felix Mendelssoh Bartholdys Wirken für den Königlichen Hof-und Domchor zu Berlin." In *Mendelssohn Studien*, vol. 16, edited by Hans-Günter Klein and Christoph Schulte, 125–137. Hannover: Wehrhahn, 2009.

Schmidt, Bernhard. *Lied – Kirchenmusik – Predigt im Festgottesdienst Friedrich Schleiermacher.* Berlin: Walter de Gruyter, 2002.

Schubert, Anselm. "Liturgie der heiligen Allianz: Die liturgischen und politischen Hintergründe der preußischen *Kirchenagende (1821/22).*" *Zeitschrift für Theologie und Kirche* 110, no. 3 (2013), 291–315.

Signale für die musikalische Welt 14 (April 1944).

Staehelin, Martin. "Der frühreife Felix Mendelssohn Bartholdy: Bemerkungen zu seinem 'Konfirmationsbekenntnis.'" In *Mendelssohn-Studien*, vol. 16, edited by Hans-Günter Klein and Christoph Schulte, 11–50. Hannover: Wehrhahn, 2009.

Stokes, Laura. "Music and Cultural Politics during the Reign of Friedrich Wilhelm IV." PhD diss., Indiana University, 2016.

Strauß, Friedrich. *Das evangelische Kirchenjahr*. Berlin: Jonas, 1850.

The Theatrical Observer, November 2, 1850. London: C. Harri, 1850.

Todd, R. Larry. *Mendelssohn: A Life in Music*. New York: Oxford University Press, 2003.

[Various Editors]. *Musica sacra*. Berlin: Mortiz Westphal; Bote & Bock, 1839– [ca. 1896].

Winterfeld, Carl von. Der evangelische Kirchengesang und sein Verhältnis zu Kunst des Tonsatzes. 3 vols. Leipzig: Breitkopf und Härtel.

Cambridge Elements ≡

Elements in Music and Musicians 1750–1850

Simon P. Keefe

University of Sheffield

Simon P. Keefe is James Rossiter Hoyle Chair of Music at the University of Sheffield. He is the author of four books on Mozart, including *Mozart in Vienna: the Final Decade* (Cambridge University Press, 2017) and *Mozart's Requiem: Reception, Work, Completion* (Cambridge University Press, 2012), which won the Marjorie Weston Emerson Award from the Mozart Society of America. He is also the editor of seven volumes for Cambridge University Press, including *Mozart Studies* and *Mozart Studies 2*. In 2005 he was elected a life member of the Academy for Mozart Research at the International Mozart Foundation in Salzburg.

About the series

Music and Musicians, 1750-1850 explores musical culture in the late eighteenth and early nineteenth centuries through individual, cutting-edge studies (c. 30,000 words) that imaginatively re-think a period traditionally associated with high classicism and early. The series interrogates images and reputations, composers, instruments and performers, critical and aesthetic ideas, travel and migration, and music and social upheaval (including wars and conflicts), thereby demonstrating the cultural vibrancy of the period. Through discussion of musicians' interactions with one another and with non-musicians, real-world experiences in and outside music, evolving reputations, and little studied career contexts and environments, Music and Musicians, 1750-1850 works across the conventional 'silos' of composer, genre, style, and place, as well as in many instances across the (notional) 1800 divide. All contributions appeal to a wide readership of scholars, students, practitioners and informed musical public.

Cambridge Elements ≡

Elements in Music and Musicians 1750–1850

Elements in the series

Dr. Charles Burney and the Organ
Pierre Dubois

The Age of Musical Arrangements in Europe 1780–1830
Nancy November

Mendelssohn and the Genesis of the Protestant A Cappella Movement
Siegwart Reichwald

A full series listing is available at: www.cambridge.org/eimm